# My Grandma's Health Secrets Revealed

*221 Home Remedies*

*I cannot emphasise strongly enough that nobody can treat, heal or cure a person just by giving general advice or their opinion. Therefore, what you read in this book is just food for thoughts.*

*~ Natasha Lukin*

# My Grandma's Health Secrets Revealed

*221 Home Remedies*

**Natasha Lukin**

Copyright © 2018 (Natasha Lukin)
All rights reserved worldwide.

No part of the book may be copied or changed in any format, sold, or used in a way other than what is outlined in this book, under any circumstances, without the prior written permission of the publisher.

Publisher: Inspiring Publishers,
P.O. Box 159, Calwell, ACT Australia 2905
Email: publishaspg@gmail.com
http://www.inspiringpublishers.com

 A catalogue record for this book is available from the National Library of Australia

National Library of Australia Cataloguing-in-Publication entry

Author: Natasha Lukin
Title: My Grandma's Health Secrets revealed
Genre: Health
ISBN: 978-0-6483865-8-2

*The natural and folk therapy treatments are easily available and simple to use.*

**The benefits of home remedies are:**

- Easy to get. Natural home remedies include common substances like salt, vinegar, bicarbonate of soda or vodka as well as herbs, vegetables, fruits and spices.

- Easy to make. A preparation of natural remedies at home such as tinctures, infusions and decoctions usually requires no special equipment.

- Not harmful. As most of those remedies are also good for cooking, they are not poisonous or contaminated with harmful chemicals (hopefully).

- Wide coverage. Natural home remedies treat a broad spectre of minor illnesses: from heartburn, diarrhea or back pain to bad breath, leg crumps, bleeding gums, sore throat or indigestion.

- Biological relevance. The active substances of plants and the physiologically active substances of the body are relevant to each other and not contradictory versus how it could be with artificially created chemicals.

# PREFACE

*"When a plant's leaves are turning brown you don't paint the leaves green. You look at the cause of the problem. If only we treated our bodies the same way".*
*Dr. Frank Lipman*

*My friends and fellow travellers,*

*Have you ever seen your kitchen benchtop as if it is your medicine cabinet? I do, and so shall you. Don't be confused by the word 'kitchen'. Your kitchen benchtop is your pharmacy at hand. Because you can find lots of natural medicinal items – if you know what they are and how to use them.*

*Let's start with the basic ones: salt, soda, Iodine, vodka, pepper, vinegar, onion, garlic, and a variety of herbs, roots and dry fruit. Some of those herbs you buy for cooking, others have been bought specifically for healing. Or you may grow them in your second 'medicine cabinet' – your veggie patch in a courtyard or on your balcony or even on your windowsill.*

*I invite you to my 'kitchen pharmacy at hand'.*

*This book is your concise self-help 'manual' on what you can do before turning to heavier weapons: over-the-counter or prescribed medications.*

*Mother Nature has been generous to us from the beginning of time, providing means for treating many health conditions. But the more expensive and often harmful chemicals in our medicine cabinets the less we use Mother Nature's gifts.*

*What is remarkable, in a strange way, that most of us know those natural secrets but there is an enormous gap between what we know and what we do, isn't it? One of the reasons is that the natural remedies take time to do their job and bring up the result. It is much easier to succumb to a temptation to use something 'fast'. We are getting so attached to 'fast foods', 'fast fixing of anything', 'fast pain reliefs', and so on. We turn a blind eye on what it costs us in a sense of a possibility of harmful side effects. We just want it NOW, no matter what. True?*

*I know that you know that – but the question remains – do we follow what we know or we just grab something from a chemist not giving much thought to it?*

*Why? Because it is 'fast'. We live in the world of fast food, fast trains, fast introductions, fast marriages and divorces, fast changes of heart.*

*When it comes to healing and treatment, it doesn't work that way. Your body will appreciate a bit of patience and proper reasoning, and foresee consequences – not the promising ones in some instances.*

> *I have based my choices on simplicity, affordability and availability.*

*I know, of course, that time is the most precious commodity. We don't want to waste time. Our brain, our lifestyle dictates us to move faster and faster, but biology of the human body doesn't catch up with that speed as yet. It needs time for providing you with a better result.*

*I give you a visual example. Imagine someone decide to swallow his whole bowl of hot soup in one gulp. What is going to happen? He either spill it over his face and body – a good case scenario, or he will chokebore with enormous amount of hot liquid that he tries to swallow – and in the worst case scenario he even might die.*

*My message to you is just a reminder that there are many better, healthier and much cheaper ways to healing than go straight to powerful but sometimes poisonous man-made chemicals.*

*In my field of expertise, I consider home remedies to be not the only things like herbs, essences, natural therapies or folk medicine but also activities you can do to improve your health. I have based my choices on simplicity, affordability and availability.*

*Nowadays, it is so easy to just go Google and find the list, for example, of those natural wonders of bicarbonate of soda. And learn about many other wonderful substances with proven healing properties that are just sitting on your benchtop.*

*I'd like to start off with some home remedies that are already there: right in front of your eyes - on your benchtop or in your pantry.*

# SYNOPSIS

This book is offering simple and easily affordable natural solutions that are readily available for treating many common ailments without leaving your kitchen, your backyard or your veggie patch.

The benefits of using natural health remedies quickly become obvious when you start implementing them into your lifestyle.

In a nutshell, they are:

- Created by Mother Nature.

- All natural.

- No harm or side effects.

- Cheaper on a budget.

- Treat common conditions the way Mother Nature intended.

Plus, they are:

- Easy to get. Natural home remedies include common substances like salt, vinegar, bicarbonate of soda or vodka as well as herbs, vegetables, fruits and spices.

- Easy to make. A preparation of natural remedies at home such as tinctures, infusions and decoctions usually requires no special equipment.

- Not harmful. As most of those remedies are also good for cooking, they are not poisonous or contaminated with harmful chemicals (hopefully).

- Wide coverage. Natural home remedies treat a broad spectre of minor illnesses: from heartburn, diarrhea or back pain to bad breath, leg crumps, bleeding gums, sore throat or indigestion.

- Biological relevance. The active substances of plants and the physiologically active substances of the body are relevant to each other and not contradictory versus how it could be with artificially created chemicals.

# Table of content

**PREFACE** ..............................................................
**SYNOPSIS** ............................................................

**SHOKING SIMPLICITY OF HEALING WITH SALT AND BICARBONATE OF SODA** ............ 19
**SALT** ........................................................... 20
**A Myth about salt** ....................................... 21
    Danger of low salt content ............................ 23
**More about salt** ........................................... 26
**How to use salt as an anti-bacterial agent** .... 27
    Treating cuts and wounds ............................ 27
    Clearing nasal passages ............................... 29
    Salt heals insect bites ................................... 30
    Light poisoning ............................................ 30
    Salt baths .................................................... 30

**BICARBONATE OF SODA** .................... 33
**12 amazing healing properties of**
**Bicarbonate of soda** .......................... 35
**7 amazing properties of Bicarbonate of**
**soda for household use** ..................... 38

**VINEGAR** ............................................ 41
**Vinegar as Medicine** ........................... 43
**Vinegar in skin and hair care** .............. 45
**Vinegar for your garden** ..................... 48

**VODKA** ............................................... 49
**Vodka as Medicine** ............................. 52
**Vodka-base home remedies** ............... 55
**Anti-cold cocktails:** ........................... 55
    Vodka, Cloves and Chilli ................... 55
    Tincture of vodka with radish ........... 56
    Cinnamon, black pepper, vodka ........ 56
    Warming drink with honey ................ 57
    Vodka, hot milk and honey ............... 58
**How to use chilli or peppercorn tincture**
**externally** ......................................... 59

**IODINE** .............................................. 61
**How to check you Iodine level** ............ 63

## GARLIC AND ONION ................................. 65
### Garlic: .................................................... 66
- Garlic and lemon water ................................ 67
- Killer of Extra Kilos ..................................... 68
- Garlic husk – look younger for longer ............ 69
- Garlic husk drink ......................................... 70

### Onion: ..................................................... 71
- Onion syrup for cough ................................. 72
- Why you should not chuck onion husks into rubbish bin ............................................. 73
- Fighting the cough ...................................... 75
- Treating skin conditions ............................... 75
- Help with edema and varicose disease ........... 76
- Natural hair growth booster ......................... 77
- Food colouring ............................................ 77
- Great for plants as well ................................ 78

## KITCHEN HERBS THAT HEAL ..................... 79
### Healing power of Coriander ........................ 80
- Anti-inflammatory Smoothies ....................... 81
- Water with coriander essential oil ................. 82

### Parsley lotion ........................................... 82
### Flax seeds against parasites ...................... 83

**HEALING HAND FOR COMMON CONDITIONS** .................... 85

**High Blood Pressure** ........................................ 86

   'Nine Forces' against high blood pressure ....... 86

   Another herbal tincture for controlling high blood pressure ........................................ 88

   Two ingredients' herbal tincture .................... 89

   Watermelon against hypertension ................. 89

   Other home remedies for controlling blood pressure ............................................. 90

   Heart candy ................................................. 91

**SIX RECIPES FOR BRAIN VESSEL CLEANSING** ........................................ 92

   1. Herbal infusion for brain vessels cleansing .. 93

   2. Preparation for brain vessels restoration base on pine needles ..................................... 94

   3. Brain vessel cleansing with garlic ............... 95

   4. Lemon, orange and honey remedy .............. 96

      Ruby grapefruit solution ........................... 96

   6. "Elixir of life" ............................................. 97

**ACUTE AND CHRONIC COUGH** ..................... 98
    Black radish with honey –
    super-expectorant, and more ........................ 98
    Tincture of vodka with radish ..................... 100
    "Nine Forces" against Cough and Asthma .... 100
    Great News on Coughing and Chocolate ....... 101
    Cabbage juice with honey ............................ 103
    Warming up ................................................ 103

**ARTHRITIS, OSTEOARTHRITIS (ARTHROSIS)
AND SIMILAR CONDITIONS** ....................... 104
    Pain relief for Arthrosis ................................ 105
    Salvation for Your Knee Joints ..................... 106
    Cabbage for bruises or inflammations
    of joints ....................................................... 108

**GENERAL HEALTH AND LONGEVITY** ......... 109
**Two Ingredients – 16 Healing Effects** ......... 110
**The Easiest Remedy to Rejuvenate
Your Body in 40 Days** ................................... 113
**The Plant of "Eternal Youth"** ...................... 115
**Lecithin, a super-charger for your brain.** 11710

**Amazing study reveals more about Omega 3 fatty acids**.................... 121
   Omega-3s and Your Memory........................122
   What Omega-3 Will Do For
   Your Brain and Body ......................................123
   How to Get Your Omega-3 ............................124

**11 CUCUMBER STORIES**............................. 125
**17 CABBAGE STORIES** ................................ 131
**MORE OF MY GRANDMA'S MEDICINE** ....... 141

**BONUS STORIES** .......................................... 145
**Why are you not losing weight?** .................. 146
**Your body is a self-healing system**.............. 150
**The ageing of the human body begins in his legs, and that is why**............................ 154
**The Mona Lisa Smile**..................................... 156
   11 steps to practice internal smile ................158
**Support for your vision** ................................ 160

# SHOKING SIMPLICITY OF HEALING WITH SALT AND BICARBONATE OF SODA

## SALT

Salt is the only natural compound of minerals that can be directly absorbed by the body. It is considered one of the most important substances, since it is necessary for the vital activity of all living beings.

Salt is the oldest food seasoning, but it has never been just a product. Since ancient times it was a substance of a higher regard, and some fights broke out because of salt. In the past the states, on the territory of which the salt roads ran, imposed huge taxes on merchants.

In ancient times, salt was given to officials and soldiers as a salary. In ancient Rome, several pieces of this mineral could be exchanged for a slave, and in the states of Central Africa salt was equal in weight to gold - one to one. The absence or sudden increase in the price of this mineral led to uprisings and a change of rulers - it suffices to recall the famous "salt riots" in Russia in 17th century.

*Everything in Nature is either medicine or poison. The essence is determined by the dose and the regimen.*

## A Myth About Salt

Salt! Did someone tell you it is bad for you, and you believe it?

Let me ask you then: have you ever taste your tears or your blood? Are they sweet, sour, bitter or….

Of course your tears could be, figuratively speaking, sweet or bitter (not sure about sour though), but they taste salty, right? And same with the blood.

Can we put two and two together?

Let me tell you: Salt is a part of our body chemical makeup. That is an undeniable fact.

Of course, there are some medical conditions when the salt intake must be drastically reduced or totally avoided.

We don't discuss that. We talk about us, 'average' people.

If you or especially older people like your parents or grandparents complain about feeling of fatigue or sometimes dizziness there is a chance that your doctor would attribute it to the fact that you are "getting older". However, the real culprit could be a low level of sodium in the blood, called Hyponatraemia.

Several years ago, research showed that a surprising number of seniors suffer from this condition. It occurs because many people - not just the older ones but younger as well - have avoided salt

throughout their lives, having been told it was a cause of high blood pressure. However, on the contrary, low sodium intake may actually increase a risk of heart attack and death.

In my practice, working with clients of various ages, I have constantly warned them against not having enough salt in their diet. However, many of them are understandably sceptical. I tried to persuade them to start using salt, not overdoing it, of course, but - with little success.

## Danger of low salt content

And this is a real story of Bernadette.

*One day, Bernadette, one of my clients who had not been well for a long while, went for a medical check-up where she was given a diagnosis of Hyponatraemia. She was in a complete shock. For so many years Bernadette stubbornly avoided salt like the plague, thinking she was doing the right thing for her health—and now she was paying the price.*

*Her symptoms included nausea and vomiting, headaches, confusion, loss of energy, drowsiness and fatigue, restlessness and irritability, muscle weakness, spasms and cramps in her legs. Fortunately, she did not experience seizures and did not fall into coma, which are also on the list of the symptoms.*

*She attributed those symptoms to "getting older" and did not bother with them for a while until she really began to crumble.*

*That was a revelation she would not want to know. She was put on appropriate medicine, however, it took her quite a while to accept her diagnosis. We talked over the issue again and again until it sank into her head. Gradually she started added a pinch of salt to her food and did not really like it. Her taste buds were not familiar with saltiness, so she was not happy to change her eating habit. But this time she had no choice.*

And now, read the quote, in which researches from internationally acclaimed Mayo Clinic (USA) explain Hyponatraemia:

"Hyponatremia occurs when the concentration of sodium in your blood is abnormally low. Sodium is an electrolyte, and it helps regulate the amount of water that's in and around your cells.

*In Hyponatremia, one or more factors — ranging from an underlying medical condition to drinking too much water — cause the sodium in your body to become diluted. When this happens, your body's water levels rise, and your cells begin to swell. This swelling can cause many and varied health problems, from mild to life-threatening".*

Another scientist, Dr McCarron, a research professor at the University of California, stated in his reports on this subject:

*"There's currently no reliable evidence that supports the recommendation to reduce intake of salt for heart health. My view is that it is very likely that low salt will ultimately prove to be another public health disaster. There is already sufficient evidence to suggest that low salt could actually result in an increased risk of cardiovascular disease."*

## What my Grandma taught me:

*Not enough salt — easy to top it up, too much salt — your forehead will be hit with a wooden spoon.*

The permanent right amount of salt in the body makes it strong and invulnerable. It strengthens its immune defences and therefore, people are not subjected to colds and flu, as well as to infectious diseases.

## More about salt

> *The cure for anything is salt water:*
> *sweat, tears or the sea.*
>
> Isak Dinesen

This is a remarkable story that happened during the WW2, regarding antiseptic property of salt:

*In Russian military hospitals there was a shortage of antibiotics and other medications. Far up North of European part of Russia surgeons began to use salty water from the Barents sea as a natural bactericidal solution. That was like a natural saline solution and it saved hundreds of soldiers' lives. After a few days under saline bandages, wounds would be cleared of puss and high fevers subsided.*

The fact is that the saline solution absorbs discharge with its pathogenic microbial content, and sucks out all the dirt and toxins, clearing the wounds. With all the arsenal of medications available from the chemist, we tend not to bother with natural solutions. But health-conscious people often ask themselves: what are the actual content of these medications? Are they based on hormones, antibiotics or strong chemicals? Are they human-friendly substances? How do we know? In my view, it is time to get back to basics.

The natural and folk therapy treatments are easily available and simple to use. Saline solution can relieve inflammation, clear your nose and throat, and heal cuts and wounds. It is easy to prepare. Just dissolve salt in water in ratio 1:10. That solution can be used for cleaning wounds and injuries, gargling and clearing the nose.

## How to use salt as an anti-bacterial agent

### Treating cuts and wounds

Apply a cloth saturated in a saline solution[*] of tepid temperature directly on the injured area.

---

[*] Saline solution is a mixture of salt and water. Normal saline solution contains roughly 1% sodium chloride (salt), which is similar to the sodium concentration in blood and tears. Saline solution is usually called normal saline, but it's sometimes referred to as physiological or isotonic saline solution.

You can make a saline solution yourself, which is easy and simple. All you need is water (Filtered prefer but tap water will do) and table salt or fine sea salt in proportion: 2 cups of water for 1 teaspoon of salt.

Mix it until dissolved and then either (1) microwave it for 1-2 minutes or (2) boil it on a stove, also for a few minutes.

The stovetop method is more sterile than the microwave one, because the boiled water could destroy pathogenic flora better.

For both methods let the solution cool down and refrigerate it in an airtight container for up to 24 hours. (After that, it should be discarded)

The cloth soaked in saline solution should not be too wet, just damp. Apply it to injured area, then cover it with Gladwrap and fix with a bandage. Leave it overnight, and then remove in the morning.

As an anti-bacterial agent salt would clean the wound and support healing process. Repeat if needed.

## Clearing nasal passages

For rinsing nasal passages and eliminating its discharge do it the yoga way. Pour a bit of saline in a saucer, close one nostril with your finger and draw in the solution into your second nostril. Meaning, you take it in through one nostril and let it out through another one. It takes a bit of practice to do it. Such procedure refreshes the internal mucous lining and supports better breathing. In yoga practices, it is recommended as a preventive and cleansing measure for protecting our respiratory system.

### Salt heals insect bites

A gruel made from 1 teaspoon of salt and a small amount of water helps reduce pain and itching, and also prevents swelling at the bite site.

### Light poisoning

If the person feels sick the best thing is to make the first cleaning - cause vomiting, for which he would need a drink of warm salted water (up to 4 to 5 glasses). Apart of provoking vomiting, saline water compensates for the loss of fluid, and removes toxic products and poisons from the body. However, depending of the severity of the condition you have to decide whether a doctor's visit or even ambulance is needed. But for this you need to make the first cleaning - cause vomiting, for which you need to drink warm salted water (4 to 5 glasses).

### Salt baths

Having a salt bath is an excellent remedy for a wide variety of ailments. Such baths enhance the skin's blood supply, and then harmful substances and toxins are eliminated from the body. Here are some examples of salt baths that you can do at home. The common thing for them: it is necessary to take a bath for 15–20 minutes at a water temperature of 36–38 ° C.

For the treatment of conditions affecting your joints and spinal column, try a salt bath. It is not just healing but very pleasant as well.

Use any salt – cooking salt, sea salt or the Himalayan one - in the ratio of 2 kg of salt per full bath (about 100 litres of water). Take a bath every other day for 10-15 minutes. Course — 10–12 sessions. Salt bath is also helpful in healing rashes, pimples and other defects of the skin.

Don't use soap in the salt bath. Finish the procedure with ringing yourself with a little bit colder pure water. Then dry yourself and the best thing after that – go to bed.

**In addition:** how to use water (with or without salt) for hydration of your skin? When we talk about moisturising and hydration and buy expensive cosmetic for that purpose, it seems to me we forget that 'moisture' and 'hydro' are about WATER. That is the best moisturising and hydration solution directly created for us by Mother Nature. But there is an important detail: to get a result we need to use good quality water to wash our face. However, the trick is not to wipe it dry straight away. Let it dry out naturally allowing your skin to absorb the liquid and get hydrated. You can also try a saline but see how your skin reacts to it. Maybe dilute it twice more.

Sounds too simple? It works for me. Maybe, it is worth trying by you as well.

# BICARBONATE OF SODA — A MIRACLE MINERAL

In the human body, in animals and plants, the role of soda is to neutralize acids, increase the alkaline reserves of the body in the maintenance of an acid-base balance in the norm. In humans, the pH value of the blood should be within the range of 7.35-7.47. If the pH is less than 6.8 (very acid blood, the strongest acidosis), then the death of the organism is imminent.

As I mentioned above, the first exceptionally useful property of soda is that it alkalizes the body. As many foods are acidic, alkalizing process could be as simple as having a quarter of teaspoon of soda with warm water before sleep.

As an example: a half of a teaspoon in hot milk with honey soothes a sore throat and reduces cough. Also gargling with soda and salt mixed together in warm water helps to recover faster.

Nowadays, the efficacy of the bicarbonate of soda for treating many conditions and ailments has been confirmed in an ample scope of reputable research.

## 12 amazing healing properties of Bicarbonate of soda

1. Baking soda is commonly used as an antacid. It effectively reduces the acidity of the stomach. If heartburn occurs, mix a teaspoon of soda in a glass of water. However, it is recommended rather as an emergency treatment than for everyday use.

2. A half of a teaspoon in hot milk with honey soothes a sore throat and reduces cough. Also gargling with soda and salt mixed together in warm water helps to recover faster.

3. Gargling with soda also works as a first aid to cure a toothache, pharyngitis or laryngitis.

*Medicinal properties of soda were known since ancient times, when it was called "the ashes of the sacred fire."*

4. You can also put a baking soda solution in a steam inhaler and breath in the vapour to treat a cough or other respiratory problems.

5. Soda can whiten your teeth, removing a deeply ingrained plaque from tea, coffee and cigarettes. Use it on your toothbrush by itself or together with a toothpaste.

6. Baking soda relieves skin irritation and itching from insect bites. For this, it is necessary to make a paste with soda and apply it to the irritated areas of the skin. This remedy is effective even on wasp and bee stings.

7. Baking soda can be used for the treatment of burns by flame, hot surfaces or acid. Simply rinse the affected area with a baking soda solution, then cover it with a cloth soaked in the same solution.

8. Soda works well when applied topically to treat haemorrhoids, an inflammation of the fingers (whitlow), conjunctivitis, fungal infections and eczema.

9. A teaspoon of soda in a glass of water is helpful managing heartbeats at arrhythmia attacks.

10. Can be applied to the underarms to rid them of unpleasant odour-causing bacteria.

11. An effective remedy for severe inflammation: sprinkle inflamed areas with baking soda. Soak a sheet with soap and stick to the foot, attach a piece of cloth on top and gently fix. Apply at night for 3 days in a row, then for 2 days take a break. Repeat if necessary.

12. Baking soda is perfect in replacing expensive bath salts. This bath will have a strong anti-inflammatory effect. If you are tired and the state of your nervous system leaves

much to be desired, then simply pour a few tablespoons of soda into the water and add a little of your favorite essential oil. A beneficial effect will not keep you waiting. After taking such a bath you will feel the softness and smoothness of your skin and pleasant relaxation.

## 7 amazing properties of Bicarbonate of soda for household use

1. Baking soda easily destroys any smells. For example, in a freezer and refrigerator, a rubbish bin, a shoe cupboard, a car and a cat's tray. To prevent the appearance of an unpleasant smell, you just need to sprinkle a solution of soda in these places.

2. With the help of soda, you can clean almost all surfaces: stainless steel, sinks, tubs, tiles and chrome. It is very effective and totally environmentally friendly.

3. If necessary, soda can replace hair shampoo. Simply mix the soda with water until a paste-like consistency is obtained, apply to the hair and rinse thoroughly. Your hair will become shiny, clean and soft.

Soda perfectly removes the remains of varnish and other fixing agents from the hair.

4. You can use soda to care for your pet. If the animal does not have time to bathe, spray the soda solution onto the hair, and then comb it. Dog's wool after such a procedure will stop stinking, become smooth and look clean.

5. You can add a glass of soda when washing. It enhances the effect of detergent, softens water and helps to preserve the color of things or whiteness in the laundry. It acts like the famous brands. So why waste extra money?

6. Do you have your own swimming pool? In this case, soda will help restore the normal acid-base balance to it. And such a problem as the "flowering" of water will disappear by itself. Soda is safe for the skin and eyes. Therefore, in the pool, which added soda, you can splash as long as you want.

7. Soda instantly extinguishes the fire. So always keep it near the stove. If you have something caught fire when frying, then just pour a handful of soda into the area of fire.

o *Attention to the pregnant women! You shall use only soda for your household cleaning needs. It has zero toxicity, and will not bring any harm to your child.*

# VINEGAR

Let's start with remembering that vinegar is the most ancient food acid. The word 'vinegar' originated from Old French vinaigre, from vin "wine" (from Latin vinum; see wine) + aigre "sour". In Latin, it was vinum acetum "wine turned sour." It was used in Ancient Greece as well, and the Greeks called it 'oxys' and it transposed into modern Russian language as "Ooksus".

In ancient Egypt vinegar was an expensive and valuable product and Cleopatra prepared a special drink based on vinegar. By dissolving pearls in it, she believed that it became 'an elixir of Youth'.

Avicenna, a Persian polymath who is known as one of the most significant physicians, astronomers, thinkers and writers of the Islamic Golden Age, has been regarded as "the father of early modern medicine". He wrote that the vinegar in Middle Eastern countries was made from grapes, sultanas, sugar, dates, honey, rice and other products.

*That majestic solution is a well of vitamins, mineral salts and microelements.*

So, what is the chemistry of the vinegar? It is a result of fermentation of lactic acid bacteria and depending on the raw material could be alcoholic, wine, fruit-berry, beer or honey vinegar.

> **What my Grandma taught me:**
> *Varicose veins in sight – rub them with apple cider vinegar.*

An usual table vinegar could be 3-, 6- and 9% solution, that means that it contains 3-, 6- or 9 grams of acetic acid in 100 grams of the liquid.

Currently, the apple cider vinegar is the most popular of all vinegars, both commercially and home made. There are a few good books of it amazing healing property of it that I found to be scientifically credible and practically useful.

## Vinegar as Medicine

Readily available the vinegar is widely known for its unique healing properties. What could be treated with the vinegar at home?

### Relieve muscle pain

After active physical exertion, muscle pain often occurs. To get rid of it do the following:

- dissolve 1 tbsp of vinegar in 100 ml of water,
- moisten a napkin,
- apply the compress on the pain zone for about 30 minutes.

### Shorten the healing time

Vinegar will shorten the healing time and ease the pain when you stretch your muscles. To do this, follow this advice:

- make a solution by mixing 500 ml of warm apple cider vinegar, 4 drops of iodine and 2 teaspoons of salt.
- wrap a sore spot with a cloth soaked in this solution.

This solution can be stored for a long time.

### Eliminate itching after insect bites

To do this, moisten a cotton ball in vinegar and place it on the bite.

### Fighting fungal infection in feet

Not that fast and easy, but with regular use the vinegar will help get rid of fungal infection on your feet. To do this, prepare a warm footbath with the addition of vinegar (1 part vinegar and 5 parts water). Take a 15-20 minute bath for a week or two until you see results. It also works for getting rid of unpleasant feet odour.

### Soothing agent for the sore throat

With mild pain, you can gurgle your sore throat with a solution prepared from 100 ml of warm water and 1 teaspoon of apple cider vinegar. Do it repeatedly throughout the day, every hour or so. If the pain subsides, keep doing it for another day however, not so often.

## Vinegar in skin and hair care

To support skin elasticity and tonus mix 2 teaspoon of vinegar with 200 ml of good water, poor it into ice forms and refrigerate. Use those ice cubes for cleaning your face and neck.

In the skin of your hands is coarse mix apple vinegar with equal amount of hand cream and rub this mixture onto your hands before going to bed.

The following facemask will rejuvenate and regenerate your skin.

**To do this:**

- mix one egg yolk with 1 tbsp. of apple vinegar, 1 tbsp. of olive oil and 2 tbsp. of grated cucumber,
- apply to your face, neck and décolleté,
- wash it out after half an hour.

One more facemask is suitable for inflamed skin and acne.

**To do this mix:**

- 1 tbsp. of oatmeal
- 1 tbsp. of honey
- 1 tbsp. of apple cider vinegar

mix them to a homogeneous consistency, apply to the face, hold for 30 minutes, then rinse.

Do it weekly for better result.

It is very common to use vinegar for rinsing hair after washing it. That makes hair more healthy and shinier.

**To do this:**

- dissolve 100 ml of apple cider vinegar in 1 liter of water,
- rinse the hair with it.

The solution will help remove the remnants of chemical preparations (shampoos, balms, masks) from the surface of the hair, improve hair quality and give them shine.

## Vinegar for your garden

- Vinegar can be successfully used in the garden to fight against aphids. To prepare the solution to spray on your plants, dissolve in 1 l of water 1 tbsp. of vinegar and use it for a few days in a row.
- Vinegar can also be beneficial for the plants, which are more appreciative of acid soil. To stimulate flowering of gardenia, azaleas and some other flowers you just need to dissolve 3 tbsp. of vinegar in 4 litres of water, and water with it the plants once a week. However, immediately after the beginning of flowering, watering with acetic solution must be stopped.

# VODKA

> *The word 'vodka' has been firmly fused with the Russians and Russia in the mind of people*

It's a subject for jokes and malicious remarks for those who practice mocking and sneering. However, this is from the same set, asserting that bears walk along the streets of Moscow, and kangaroos freely skip the streets of Sydney.

Therefore, I wish to share with you a bit of history of VODKA.

Although vodka has always been considered a national alcoholic beverage in Russia, in ancient times Russian people consumed only low-alcohol drinks, infused with honey, herbs or roots. People also liked to sip berry wine or freshly brewed beer. Drinks were made at home and exhibited on a large table during the holidays. A great sobriety was required from the people and the nobility, and the drunkards seen in gluttony were imprisoned - first for a short time, and if they did not correct, they would be publicly lashed on the street.

The term "vodka" first appeared in the XIV century, but denoted it as a berry or herbal tincture in alcohol. In 1450, this alcoholic decoction was brought to Russia by Italian ambassadors. At this time, it was recommended as an antimicrobial substance and used to disinfect wounds and cuts. And, in turn, it came to Italy from Persia and only meant to be used as medicine.

Under Ivan the Terrible, vodka became very popular and began to be taken orally. Historians told us, that the king, seeing the possibility of easy replenishment of the treasury in the sale of alcohol, forc-

ibly and cruelly instilled the tradition of drinking in the people. Vodka was supposed to be bought in taverns and inns while home production of the tinctures was banned completely. Since then, the notorious alcohol addiction, previously unusual for a Russian person, has developed.

Unlike Ivan the Terrible, the Bolsheviks, who headed the country in 1917, imposed a prohibition law on drinking alcohol until 1924. The last General Secretary of the USSR, Mikhail Gorbachev, had issued a similar decree. However, it never stood the trial of time.

Lets leave aside the talk about heavy drinking and familiarise ourselves with how vodka could be used as medicine.

## Vodka as Medicine

Treatment of colds with vodka and chilli or pepper is one of effective remedies in natural medicine. It helps relieve pain, ease visual signs of the ailment and prevent the development of a serious illness.

Does vodka really help with colds? The answer to this question is unequivocal - yes. However the

main condition is to know and follow some rules of how to take and apply vodka properly - and strictly observe them.

The first symptoms for the treatment with vodka are:

- Tiredness and fatigue;
- Sharp or aching headache;
- General weakness;
- Running nose;
- Blocked ears.

Those symptoms manifest themselves mainly after strong hypothermia: a long walk in the cold, wet shoes or out-of-season clothing.

In this case, vodka with chilli or pepper, famously known as "**Pertsovka**", used both inside and externally. It will help to warm up instantly and prevent the development of colds.

But despite the positive properties of the infusion, it has own contraindications.

As with all the medications and remedies, certain contra-indications should be taken into consideration. Use of this particular treatment should be limited or stopped altogether in cases such as:

- Cannot be used for children because of the risk of toxic poisoning.
- The same applies to pregnancy and breast-feeding period.
- In case of individual intolerance or allergic reaction.
- Cannot be used for treating sore throat, pharyngitis and laryngitis with acute inflammatory process in the pharynx and tonsils. The effect of vodka in this case will only aggravate the patient's condition.
- High blood pressure.
- Gastrointestinal tract's conditions.

## Vodka-base home remedies

How prepare properly and take such unusual, useful remedies?

## 1. Anti-cold cocktails

They shall be taken at the first signs of the cold.

### Vodka, Cloves and Chilli

**Ingredients:**

- Pure water         1 glass
- Cloves             3 buds
- Chilli             1 pod
- Quality vodka      0.5 L

Bring water to boil. Meanwhile finely chop cloves and a chilli pod. Put it into boiling water, mix well and leave to infuse for 40 minutes. Add vodka, cover the pan and leave for 2-4 hours. Strain the prepared infusion in a glass container.

Take a tablespoon of that infusion with meals three times a day.

### Tincture of vodka with radish

The recipe for a drink is easy and does not take much time to make. This cocktail helps eliminate cough, soothes sore throat and diminishes signs of colds.

- Vodka -                         1 glass
- Black radish juice* -   10 drops
- Chilli juice* -                5 drops.

Combine the above ingredients in one container and mix them thoroughly. Take 30ml of the tincture twice a day in 30 minutes after a meal.

### Cinnamon, black pepper, vodka

Tincture effectively helps to eliminate colds, and cures sore throat and cough.

**Ingredients:**

- Black ground pepper -  1/4 tbsp
- Vodka -                             100 ml
- Ground cinnamon -        1/2 tsp.

Mix all the ingredients in a glass container. Cover it and place in a fridge for 24 hours. Strain and drink 2 tablespoons 2 times a day. The course -3 days.

---

* just grate them and squeeze drops of juice.

## Warming drink with honey

Consider the recipe of vodka with pepper and honey. Preparation doesn't take long, and the decoction provides vitamins and strengthen the immune system.

### Ingredients:

- Vodka – 0.5 L
- Natural honey - 3 tablespoons
- Chilli - 1 pod
- Cloves - 3 buds
- Pepercorn - 8 pcs.

Crash and chop chilli, cloves and peppercorn, mix with honey and cover with vodka. Mix well and let it stay as infusion for 24 hours. Take in small portions after meal.

Next one is life-saving mixture in especially severe cases of being exposed to freezing temperature:

## Vodka, hot milk and honey

**Ingredients:**

- Hot milk–        1 glass
- Vodka –          30 ml
- Honey -          1 tablespoon
- Be in bed.

Drink it fast and as hot as it is possible to drink.

Cover the person with doonah or lots of blankets, even over his head and let him sleep.

He will sweat profusely, and if awake, change his pajama and continue staying under the very warm covering.

This treatment would surely prevent the development of pneumonia or bronchitis.

# How to use chilli or peppercorn tincture externally

**Option 1.**

1. Vodka with chilli or pepper, called "**Pertsovka**," is recommended to use as a compress for relief from cough. For this, the infusion is to be diluted in a small vessel with plain water in a ratio 1:1.

2. In a prepared solution, moisten a small piece of cotton cloth and place it on the throat, then cover it with a small layer of cotton material. Fix the compress with a bandage and leave for 2-3 hours. Perform the procedure once a day. And then, before going to bed it is recommended to drink hot tea with honey for maximum effect.

**Option 2.**

This option is highly effective for bringing high temperature down. This time you need to prepare a solution of vodka with water and vinegar in equal proportions, which would be used externally for rubbing. The main condition is to follow the rules, especially if the patient has a high fever.

For rubbing, lay the patient on his back. Take a napkin or a small cut of natural tissue, moisten in the prepared solution and wipe the body with light movements. Using a hairdryer, lightly blow out over the area with warm air for 2 minutes. Then cover the patient with a blanket, and put a cold compress on his head. Keep it cool by refreshing it when it gets warm. In 30 minutes after the procedure, it is worth measuring the body temperature, which would drop, most likely. If necessary, repeat it again.

# IODINE

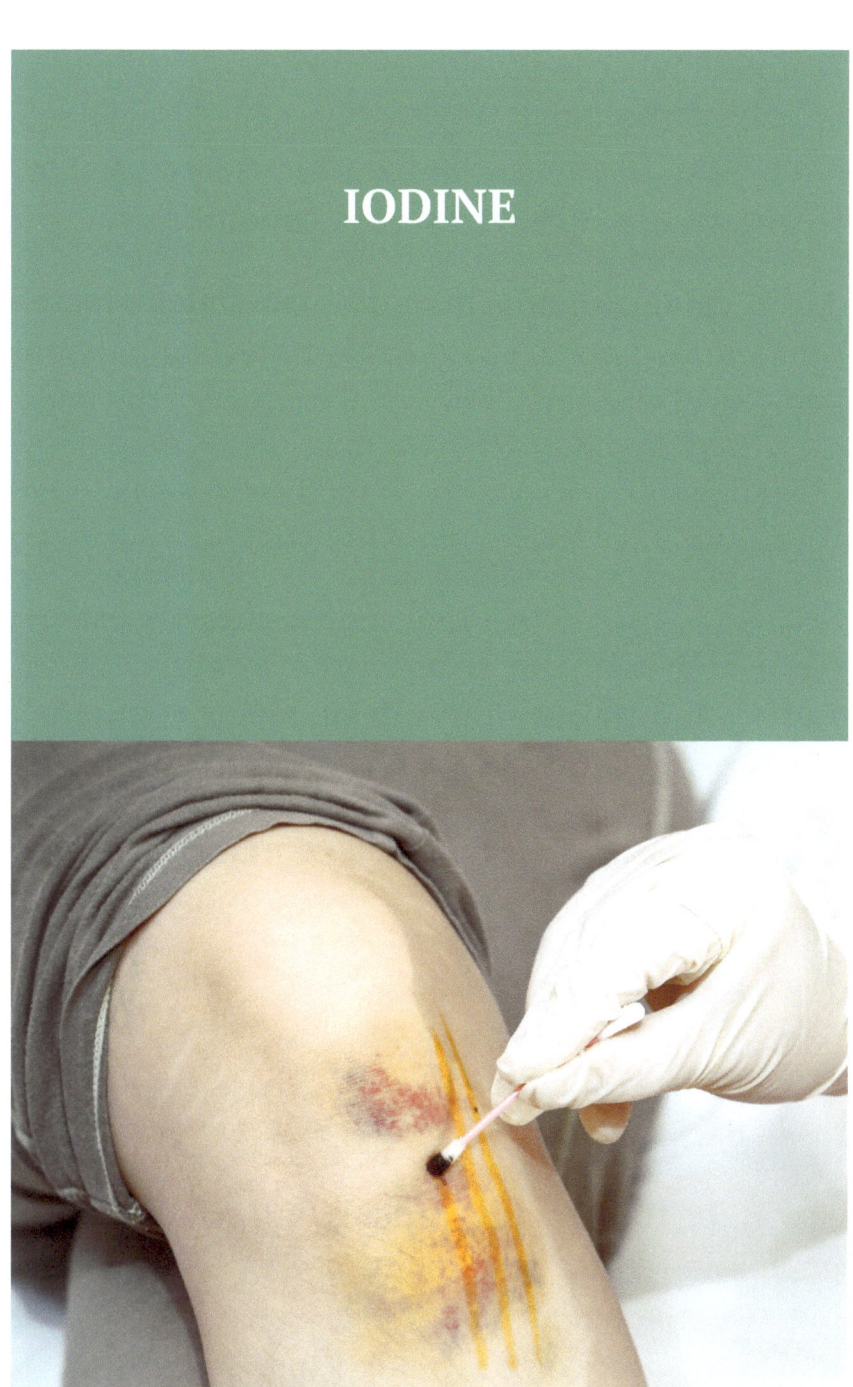

Iodine tincture in alcohol, also known as Betadine is one of the most effective and easily available antiseptics. However, Iodine can also be used for treating a whole range of other conditions.

A few inter-crossing lines (the so-called "iodine grid") drawn on the skin helps relieve an ailment because of the double effect of iodine on the body.

Firstly, iodine molecules strengthen local blood flow, creating a heat-producing effect.

Secondly, it is proven that iodine suppresses bacterial activities and reduces the intensity of inflammation by entering subcutaneous tissues via the pores.

Other conditions that could benefit from using the iodine grid include:

- Respiratory conditions
- Varicose veins
- Injuries and bruises
- Back and joint pain

According to the recent studies, one third of world population suffer from Iodine deficit, often not being aware about it. Iodine is a chemical element that is required for growth and survival.

An iodine deficiency can lead to goitre, a disease characterised by an abnormally enlarged thyroid gland, which leads to some serious health consequences.

*According to the recent studies, one third of the world population suffer from Iodine deficit.*

In developed countries, the situation might be better and people usually get enough iodine from their food. However, this may not be the case for some people with metabolic disorders or pregnant women.

## How to check you Iodine level

There is a simple method to check whether you have enough Iodine in your systems or suffer from its deficiency.

Let's do it right now, will you?

Before bedtime, rub or smear your heels with Iodine and put on socks. If in the morning your heels are still of yellowish brown colour you have nothing to worry about.

However, if your heels are pink without traces of Iodine it is pointing to the deficit of it in your body. Continue to do the procedure every night until your body satisfy with its Iodine content.

And then you start enjoying a positive 'side effects' of this home treatment. You become less irritable, more optimistic, less anxious – because those are signs of ailing thyroid gland.

Therefore, that is a test and that is a cure.

# GARLIC AND ONION

If you ask somebody to name the most useful vegetable, famous of its healing properties, half of the respondents will choose garlic, and the second half will name onions. It is common knowledge and practice to use garlic and onion as a preventive measure and in treatment of colds and flu. But that is not all, of course.

*These two vegetables are leaders among all the popular medicinal plants, practically across the world.*

## Garlic

For example, chemicals in garlic contribute to the thinning of blood, and therefore do not allow the formation of clots and improve blood flow. Regular use of garlic reduces the risk of hypertension, and also normalizes the level of glucose in the blood. For this purpose it is recommended eating one clove of garlic in the morning, before drinking your first glass of warm water.

## Garlic and lemon water

This recipe is an ancient Chinese homeopathic remedy and has been found recorded on five-thousand-year-old clay tablets. This amazing solution cleanses the body of excess fat, bad cholesterol and calcium deposits, dramatically improving metabolism. Blood vessels become non-rigid, which works to prevent heart attacks, angina, sclerosis and tumour formation. But that's not all—it can ease headaches and tinnitus and improve vision.

Peel one whole garlic bulb but don't remove the tiny, thin membranes from the cloves. Wash one lemon with boiling water and remove its rind. Put the prepared garlic and lemon rind into a blender and mix well. Put it in a glass container and cover with 600g of cooled, boiled water. Close the lid and refrigerate for 3-4 days.

Then strain the tincture and take 50g of it on an

**What my Grandma taught me:**
*Mix garlic with parsley and rub it over dermatitis.*

> *Studies revealed that garlic husks contain 4 per cent of the powerful antioxidant, bioflavonoid Quercetin.*

empty stomach in the morning every day for 3 months. Then take a break for a month.

If you follow this recipe exactly and take it regularly you will feel your body's rejuvenation.

### Killer of Extra Kilos

This is a mixture of common ingredients that burn excess fat.

- 4 cloves of garlic
- 4 small tomatoes
- 1 glass of water
- 6 ice cubes (optional)
- 6 tablespoons of lemon juice

Put all ingredients in a blender and mix well. Take this mixture 2-3 times a week, half an hour after breakfast.

Lycopene in tomatoes is a strong antioxidant that helps in removing excess fat, toxins and other impurities from your body.

The amazing properties of garlic are also great for burning calories and improving your general well-being. The mixture works its best when we observe our diet and try to avoid sugar.

## Garlic husk – look younger for longer

Don't throw your white garlic husk away—save it. It's one of the most valuable natural aids for longevity. If you drink a special concoction made of white garlic husk you will feel and look your best.

So, what is it about garlic husk? What are its healing properties?

If you look at a small piece of husk under a microscope you can see Quercetin crystals neatly laid in rows. This is a natural, biologically active substance belonging to the vitamin R group. Quercetin is now a very popular supplement that can be found in garlic, onion, apple and green tea. It is available as a supplement in health shops and chemists.

**What my Grandma taught me:**
*A slice of garlic on empty stomach –kills virus like a bullet.*

However, making your own solution costs almost nothing and you can be sure it's purely natural.

The famous Dr Atkins considered Quercetin to be the best antihistamine and prescribed it to his patients suffering from various allergies. However, Quercetin is even more popular as a preventive means for cardiovascular conditions. People who take a lot of Quercetin have a lower risk of heart attacks, strokes and blood clots forming. We can prepare two different drinks based on garlic that are beneficial in many ways.

### Garlic husk drink

To prepare this drink, take 4 glasses of water, bring to the boil and allow cool for 3 minutes. Then take 4 handfuls of garlic husk and cover with the hot water. Leave for 6-8 hours. It is best to drink all 4 glasses in one day, or at least as much as you feel you can drink.

Do this for 10 days in a row and the difference will be visible. Your skin will become smoother, radiant and younger looking. Remember, what we see externally is also happening inside the body.

## Onion

Along with garlic, onion is also the first remedy for colds. When the acute respiratory viral infection and influenza season begins, it is highly recommended to consume onions for prevention. Most people know that. But what is less known that the onion bulb can simply be cut into slices and placed on plates in the room. The phytoncides released from it disinfect the air, killing viruses and microbes.

• • • • • • • • • • • • • • • • • • • • • • • • • • • • •

*Flavonoids are powerful antioxidants with anti-inflammatory and immune system benefits.*

• • • • • • • • • • • • • • • • • • • • • • • • • • • • •

### Onion syrup for cough

To get rid of cough you can make onion syrup, which has an expectorant effect. Finely chop the onion, pour 150 ml of water and boil it. Slightly cool and add 2 tablespoons of honey. After half an hour, strain the broth and take 1 teaspoon several times a day before meals.

Those are just a few examples of garlic and onion health benefits.

However, both plants have such an ample scope of healing properties that to name them all would require volumes of descriptions. At the same time the majority of us already possess enough information on their healing powers.

So, I decided to pick some less known aspects of them and tell you about their husks. You might be surprised to learn that those husks are also of a great value for your health.

## Why you should not chuck onion husks into rubbish bin

The simple answer is: because it is a very valuable product with many useful properties. Let me introduce some of them.

Everybody knows how amazing onion is. When we say it we mean an internal bulb of the vegetable. But the onion husks have many benefits as a home remedy and not just that.

The onion husks contain fiber and ingredients that decrease a risk of cardio-vascular conditions as well as have a healing and anti-inflammatory effect on intestinal gastric tract and on the body in general.

The onion husk is rich in flavonoids, fructose and fiber.

**What my Grandma taught me:**
*The older the man the more onion for him.*

In recent years a lot of studies demonstrated an important role of flavonoids in prevention of such serious conditions like cancer, diabetes and Neurodegenerative disease.

A large-scale, 25-year study, published in 1995 in the journal Archives of Internal Medicine, looked at men across seven countries and found that flavonoid consumption was significantly associated with longevity.

The researchers suggested flavonoid consumption could account for 25 per cent of the observed difference in mortality rates from coronary heart disease and cancer.

Lets see a few examples of how the onion husks can be used as home remedy.

### Fighting the cough

This is a recipe for using an onion husks concoction as expectorant soothing strong annoying cough and supporting quicker recovery.

To prepare this remedy take 15 onion's heads, collect husks and cover it with 1 L of cold water. Bring it to boil and simmer until a half of the liquid evaporates. Then let it cool down completely, strain and drink 2 tablespoons 4-5 times a day.

### Treating skin conditions

In order to get rid of warts, small cuts, fungus and dermatitis one can use finely chopped husks mixed 2 to 3 parts with some fatty cream or Vaseline. Apply it to your damaged skin 2 times a day. Store it in a cool place.

## Help with edema and varicose disease

That recipe is to reduce pains in the legs and varicose and vein disease.

Take 2 tablespoons of the husks and 2 tablespoons of chamomile flowers. Cover with 2 glasses of water, boil the mixture for 15 minutes and leave it for up to 5-6 hours. Then simmer it until a half the water evaporates.

What is left, rub it into painful areas.

Another option is to mix finely chopped onion husks with equal amount of olive oil. Leave it for 10 days in a glass container and then use it for feet and legs massage.

> **What my Grandma taught me:**
> *Suffer from boils?*
> *Eat onion until you cry.*

## Natural hair growth booster

Very popular use of the husks is in hair care. It is widely used to support hair growth, strengthening the hair and giving it a beautiful shine.

This decoction is very easy to prepare. Just take 1 part of husks and roughly twice as much water and leave it to infuse for a few hours. Ring your hair with this infusion each time after you wash you hair. Keep doing it for a few weeks and you see a noticeable improvement.

## Food colouring

Onion husks has an excellent, harmless but healthy food colouring's property. Adding onion husks or even the whole onion, washed but with the husks intact, while cooking a chicken soup or broth, make them look more appealing and appetizing with its slight golden hue.

## Great for plants as well

The onion husks decoction can be used for rinsing indoor plants cleansing them of the mites and various bacteria. It is also works as a fertilizer. To make a decoction just take a glass full of husks, place it in 1L jar, pour boiled water over it and leave for a day. Next day strain it and clean your plants, especially the reversed side of the leaves. Next day rinse them with clean water.

That is far from the whole list of the onion husks benefits but those are easy to prepare and apply.

# KITCHEN HERBS THAT HEAL

## Healing power of Coriander

In some countries it goes under different names. For example, in Georgia, Armenia and Azerbaijan - the Caucasus Mountains' countries – people call it Kindza.

In other places it is called Cilantro or Chinese parsley, however, they are not exactly the same.

Fresh coriander contains large amounts of:

- Vitamins A, C, E, K, PP and group B,
- Minerals Potassium, Calcium, Manganese, Iron, Phosphorus and others,
- Pectin, Rutin, Alkaloids and essential oils.

> *One of the best products to remove Mercury and other heavy metals from your body is a herb known as coriander.*

Because of such natural richness Coriander is known for its anti-inflammatory, anti-bacterial, life force strengthening, detoxifying and soothing properties. That is why by having it as a part of your diet it plays a preventive role against infectious and viral illnesses.

Coriander also supports cardiovascular, nervous and respiratory systems, as well as the digestive tract's health.

It is a very good habit to have the fresh herb added to your meals. However, to get maximum benefit from coriander, the following recipes could be useful:

### Anti-inflammatory Smoothies

Chop finely 100 g coriander, add 100ml freshly made apple juice, 100 ml of water, 1 teaspoon of any sprouts. Mix it all well in a blender. Drink through your day.

### Water with coriander essential oil

The coriander essential oil is a very powerful anti-inflammatory as well as detoxifying substance. You only need 1-2 drops of this oil in a glass of water.

Drink it once daily. Research confirmed that by doing that for a month and a half the body can rid of up to 80% of heavy metals and toxins.

Warning: as always, consult your doctor before using any of natural remedies.

### Parsley lotion

A home-made lotion with parsley eliminates acne, reduces any kind of swelling or irritation, whitens, tones and refreshes the skin. It could also remove freckles. This lotion could be a great supplement in treating kidney disease and diabetes, as well as inflammation - if taken by a teaspoon before food.

**Ingredients:**

- 2 table spoons of the chopped parsley leaves
- 1 teaspoon of lemon juice or apple cider vinegar
- 200ml of water

**Preparation**:

- Boil parsley in water for 15 minutes.
- Let cool down and add lemon juice or apple cider vinegar at your choice.
- Keep it in a glass container in the fridge.

**How to use it:**

Simply apply it to a required area using your fingers. Do it regularly at least twice a day. It takes a bit of time to see the results as that is always the case with natural remedies.

## Flax seeds against parasites

Flax seeds' decoction cleanses the body of almost all parasites apart of roundworms. However, if you add a couple of cloves' buds even roundworms would not survive.

Flax seed oil is also a popular product with a specific odour. It has a lot of health benefits but its

*Flax seeds, or linseeds could be called the champions among anti-parasites products.*

anthelmintic activity is not that high as in the decoction. That is explained by the fact that the large amount of helpful substances and fiber stays in the oilcake.

To prepare decoction one need 2 tablespoons of flax seeds to one litre on water. This solution is left to simmer for 30 minutes, then stays for infusion until cooled down.

It is suggested to take between 100 and 200 ml half an hour before meal 2-3 times a day. It is desirable to exclude sugar for the period of cleansing.

To get rid of parasites the whole seeds also could be used. At the beginning of anti-parasite cleansing take 2 tablespoons on seeds twice a day for the duration of 8-10 days. They can be also used as a preventative measure on a regular basis.

The conclusion: flax seeds are powerful and easily available means to keep parasites at bay.

**What my Grandma taught me:**
*Dill seeds' infusion –
great to stop bed-wetting.*

# HEALING HAND FOR COMMON CONDITIONS

# High Blood Pressure

## 'Nine Forces' against high blood pressure

One of the very popular medicinal plants in herbal medicine is Elecampane. That is due to its healing, nearly miraculous properties. It grows widely in many regions of Russia and throughout Europe as well.

Elecampane plant has its Russian name: 'Devyasil'. That translates from the Russian language as 'Nine Forces' where 'devyat' is Nine, and 'sila' stands for the Force. In the traditional folk medicine Devyasil has been considered as a remedy 'against nine ailments'.

Devyasil is useful in treating various conditions – from high blood pressure to improving appetite and digestion, regulates secretory function of the stomach and intestines and stimulates metabolism.

This is a recipe that has been effectively used for treating high blood pressure for centuries.

To prepare this medicinal tincture you will need the following ingredients:

- 80 g of Devyasil's root
- 50g of untreated oats and
- 30 g of honey.

**How to make it:**

- First you rinse oats, cover it with 5 litres of water and bring it to boil. Then leave it for 4 hours to cool.
- Next pour that mixture over the Devyasil's roots, bring it to boil and leave for 2 hours. Then add honey.

**How to take it:** Take 1/3 of a glass 3 times a day for 2-3 weeks.

This tincture keep your arterial pressure normal, strengthen your heart muscle and regulate the cholesterol level.

### Another herbal tincture for controlling high blood pressure.

It recommended as a very effective remedy for keeping your blood pressure in normal brackets is as follows.

**Ingredients:**

- 1 tablespoon of Camomile
- 1 tablespoon of Immortelle
- 1 tablespoon of St. John's Wart
- 1 tablespoon of wild strawberry leaves
- 1tablespoon of birch tree buds

**How to make it:**

Mix the herbs together. Then take a portion, like 1-2 tablespoons of the mixture, pour over with 0.5L boiling water, cover it and leave for 2 hours.

How to take it:Take it as 30-50 ml 2-3 times a day.

### Two ingredients' herbal tincture

Only dry camomile flowers and dry St. John's Wart herb are needed.

Mix those 2 dry herbs in equal amount, 100g each, pour boiled water over the mixture – not much, like about one glass, and let it brew for 2 hours.

Take 30-50 ml of the tincture 2-3 times a day. This tincture has an important advantage as it has no contra-indications and can be used at any age.

### Watermelon against hypertension

Next is a unique fruit – a watermelon. The watermelon does not just remove excessive fluids from your body, but also is cleansing kidneys and decreasing cholesterol and, therefore, effectively

> **What my Grandma taught me:**
> *Plenty of watermelon needed – not just for blood pressure, but for Arthritis, gout and sclerosis.*

fights hypertension – high blood pressure. To use it as medicine you have to take the watermelon's skin and seeds, dry them out, grate and take one tablespoon twice a day.

That means don't throw the watermelon skin and seeds away as they could become your natural medicinal remedy.

## Other home remedies for controlling blood pressure

1. Beetroot: Mix beetroot juice with honey, and use it during the day in small portions.

2. Aloe juice: It has many medicinal properties, for both external and internal use. To use it for controlling your blood pressure delute one teaspoon of Aloe juice in 50ml of water and take it on empty stomach.

3. Brew a tea with mint or peppermint leaves. Drink it and also rub it into your neck. The aromatherapy effect could be felt while placing peppermint oil or sprigs of mint around the house.

## Heart candy

That is a 'healing candy', a real balm for the heart. Especially if you experience unpleasant feelings of Arrhythmia, Tachycardia or Bradycardia or similar conditions.

How make a heart candy at home, quickly and easily.

**Ingredient for a daily portion:**

- Flaxseeds –        1 tablespoon
- Sesame seeds –     1 tablespoon
- Poppy seeds –      1 tablespoon
- Turmeric –         ½ teaspoon
- Honey –            2 tablespoons.

**Next:**

- lightly fry sesame seeds in dry frying pan
- mix it with flaxseeds and poppy seeds
- grind it in a coffee grinder or blender
- add Turmeric to the powder
- mix it all with honey.

**Yum!**

**How to take it:**

Either mix it with yoghurt – 1 tablespoon for a cup.

Or take it as it is: 1-2 tablespoons, after drinking a glass of water.

This 'candy' contains lots of trace minerals, antioxidants, vitamins and fiber, which are good nutrients for your body, and in particular for your heart.

## SIX RECIPES FOR BRAIN VESSEL CLEANSING

As we strive for healthy longevity we need to look after our memory and our mind. Health-wise, that means taking good care of our brain's blood vessels. With time, some unwanted deposits accumulate on the inside walls, blood circulation gradually begins to experience difficulties and the workings of our brain become disrupted.

We can help using herbal remedies that we can make at home. There are a few examples of herbal infusions that demonstrate their efficacy through centuries. These remedies make our vessels soft and non-rigid, eliminate dizziness and noise in the ears, improve metabolism and support general body cleansing.

## 1. Herbal infusion for brain vessels cleansing

- 100g camomile
- 100g St John's Wort
- 100g immortelle
- 100g birch buds
- Water
- Honey
- Bay rum essential oil

Shred the herbs and mix them up. Boil half a litre of water and pour it over 1 tablespoon of the mixture, leaving it to brew for 20 minutes. Then strain it, take half of the liquid, add 1 teaspoon honey and 1 drop bay rum oil. Drink it last thing before going to sleep.

The next morning, warm up the rest of the liquid but do not re-boil. Add another teaspoon of honey and another drop of bay rum oil. Drink it 20 minutes before breakfast. Keep making this concoction and use it as above every day until all herbs are used. Like with any natural medicine, results can take time, but you should feel better after 2-3 weeks.

## 2. Preparation for brain vessels restoration base on pine needles

One more recipe came from a nurse who suggested it to some patients in the haematology ward where she worked. She also recommended it for after chemotherapy to restore the immune system, especially for kids.

This mixture covers a much wider range of conditions including kidney and cardiovascular problems, atrophy of the optic nerve, cramps in the legs and more: so strong is the power of pine needles, the main ingredient of the recipe.

**Ingredients:**

- 5 tablespoons pine needles
- 2 tablespoons crushed rosehip berries
- 2 tablespoons onion husks
- 1 litre of water

Mix the ingredients together and bring to boil—leave to brew overnight wrapped in a warm blanket.

Drink between half a litre and one litre daily.

### 3. Brain vessel cleansing with garlic

**Ingredients:**

- 1 bulb of garlic
- 1 glass of unrefined sunflower oil
- 1 lemon

Take the garlic, press it and cover with the sunflower oil, then put it in the fridge. It became garlic oil. The next day, juice the lemon. Mix one teaspoon of the garlic oil with a teaspoon of lemon juice and take it 30 minutes before meals, three times per day. However, don't mix garlic and lemon in advance. The course of this treatment is a minimum of one month.

## 4. Lemon, orange and honey remedy

This is a very useful recipe for cleansing the vessels in the brain and strengthening the immune system. Plus, it is beneficial for your nervous system. Take 2 lemons and 2 oranges—remove the pips but keep the skin—mince or blend them into a homogeneous mass. Place into a glass jar, add 2 tablespoons of honey and refrigerate. Take 2 teaspoons of this citrus honey before a meal over the course of a month. It is very tasty and full of goodness.

## 5. Ruby grapefruit solution

That is a well-known and proven method for cleansing your vessels. Grapefruit has some unique properties that make it the perfect food to enjoy while you're getting rid of the toxins in your body and cleansing your blood vessels. If you start your breakfast with a half of grapefruit, preferably the ruby one, for a month you will feel the difference.

### 6. "Elixir of life"

This is an easy recipe for cleansing the vessels, eliminating headaches and supporting general wellbeing. Take honey, olive oil and lemon juice in equal proportion (1:1:1). Mix them and take 1 teaspoon of the mixture every morning on an empty stomach, 30 minutes before breakfast—that's it.

Many people, including my friends and relatives, have used all these recipes with great success. Try them for yourself!

## ACUTE AND CHRONIC COUGH

### Black radish with honey – super-expectorant, and more

The recipe for a remedy of black radish and honey is known for many generations. It is highly efficient and can be used for treating most of the respiratory system's conditions. Bitter-tasting black radish has a large number of healing properties, and in combination with honey it becomes an excellent cough remedy.

This liquid is considered a natural antibiotic, and therefore of a great help with the flu, colds, bronchitis and laryngitis. It relieves tickling in the throat, dilutes sputum, contributes to its release from the bronchi and facilitates breathing.

The prepared remedy is a biologically active substance that destroys and inhibits the development of pathogenic bacteria. Apart from being the best expectorant, it possesses such healing property as anti-inflammatory, and antimicrobial and it stimulates the immune system.

The recipe for this natural medicine is quite simple, and everyone can prepare it at home.

## What my Grandma taught me:
*Honey, lemon, garlic mix – breathing easier at once.*

**To create this remedy, you should:**

- prepare a radish - thoroughly wash it and remove the upper part with a sharp knife;
- extract the core and create a pit or a hole in the centre of the root;
- pour a couple of tablespoons of natural honey or granulated sugar into the pit[*];
- depending on a size of the radish, set it on top of a glass, jar or bowl.
- let it stand for 4–6 hours;
- When the juice is released and mixed with honey or sugar, start taking the syrup in small portions but often;
- for continuous supply use 3-5 radishes at the same time, as the juice is coming out slowly and you might want more.

---

[*] Just do not add too much honey or sugar, since there will be no space left for the liquid that is released, and it will simply spill out.

> **What my Grandma taught me:**
> *Heal away
> sore throat pain—
> use lemon, rosehip,
> honey and good sleep.*

## Tincture of vodka with radish

The recipe for a drink is easy and does not take much time to make. This cocktail calms your cough, soothes sore throat and diminishes signs of cold.

- vodka -                 1 glass;
- black radish juice -    10 drops (grate and squeeze)
- chilli juice -          5 drops.

Combine the above ingredients in one container and mix them thoroughly.

Take 30ml of the tincture twice a day in 30 minutes after a meal.

## "Nine Forces" against Cough and Asthma

A special tea made with Elecampane, the plant known as Nine Forces helps to effectively fight cough.

**The recipe is easy to follow:**

- place teaspoon of the rhizomes of the plant into large bowl
- add a liter of boiling water and leave for fifteen minutes
- take one glass of the infusion 2-3 times during the day, along with honey.

In cases of asthma: the juice obtained from the roots and rhizomes of 'Nine Forces' combine with honey in 1 : 1 ratio, and then drink a teaspoon twenty minutes before meals three times a day.

## Great News on Coughing and Chocolate

Professor Alyn Morice from the University of Hull, a specialist of cardiovascular and respiratory diseases and his team proved that the best remedy for coughing is chocolate—specifically darker varieties with a high content of cocoa and low sugar content.

The results evidently confirmed that cocoa works better than any other cough mixtures. So, the scientists recommend eating dark chocolate regularly to help ease your cough symptoms.

The key substance responsible for this result is a chemical Theobromine, found in cocoa beans. It suppresses coughs even more effectively than Codeine, which is the main component in many cough mixtures.

To maximise the effect, melt the chocolate so it becomes a warm liquid. The hot chocolate helps to create a protective membrane in your throat. However, even a piece of chocolate will bring relief if you keep it in your mouth until it has completely melted.

## Cabbage juice with honey

By adding honey to cabbage juice, we turn it into medicine for cough, acute respiratory diseases and sore throats.

Honey enhances the expectorant and antimicrobial action of cabbage. It is diluted in half a glass of drink in 1: 1 ratio. Drink 3 times a day one hour before meals and stop after recovery.

Also, you can rinse the throat with juice and honey, but first dilute with water in proportion 1 : 1.

## Warming up

From the old folk medical books to us passed another recipe for cough compress from cabbage leaves with honey. The procedure is done at night for at least 3 days in a row. In the hot water that is about to boil, whole cabbage leaves are blanched for a few minutes. Then they are removed from boiling water, cooled to body temperature and spread with a thin layer of honey. "Honey" side, the leaves are applied to the chest and back, avoiding the heart area. The leaves are covered with film and secured with several layers of bandage, a suitable tight sweater is put over the compress. Now it's better to go to bed so that the remedy will work. In the morning it will be easier to breathe, there will be a liquefaction and discharge of sputum from the bronchi, the attacks of spasmodic cough will decrease.

**Comment:** *All the above recipes are suitable for a "wet" cough from a mild cold. With a high temperature and a dry cough, you should immediately call a doctor.*

## ARTHRITIS, OSTEOARTHRITIS (ARTHROSIS) AND SIMILAR CONDITIONS

Let us briefly clarify what those conditions are.

Arthritis is an umbrella term for several conditions - such as Rheumatoid arthritis and gout. They cause inflammation, which affect your bones, ligaments, and joints, giving us pain and joint stiffness.

In some cases, the inflammation can also affect your skin, muscles, and organs.

Arthrosis is another name for Osteoarthritis. It is the most common type of arthritis and caused by normal wear and tear on your joints and cartilage, and mostly related to ageing.

## Pain relief for Arthrosis

If in the morning your feet are aching and first steps off the bed are really difficult, that means it is likely you are 'hosting' Arthrosis in your legs.

Of course, in this case get an advice from your doctor, maybe a rheumatologist and orthopaedist. Possibly, they suggest you to use medicinal anti-arthrosis gels from the chemist.

They also might suggest that you use medical bile for compresses. And that is a credible natural remedy.

**How to do it – step by step:**

1. soak a cloth in medical bile that you can buy at the chemist shop
2. turn it around your legs, then cover it with something like Gladwrap
3. then cover it with a woollen scarf or similar
4. leave it there overnight.

**What my Grandma taught me:**
*Rub your feet with lemon – pain will be gone rather quickly*

> **What my Grandma taught me:**
> *Black radish juice to rub in joints – fights rheumatism and gives relief.*

Do such compresses every second day, and you are supposed to reduce your morning discomfort significantly.

And, of course, you have to move, walk and don't allow your legs to get lazy. What is also helpful for the legs is a contrast douche alternating hot and cold water.

That elevates muscle tonus, improves circulation and – hence! – a postponement of the body ageing.

## Salvation for Your Knee Joints

One of the most common complaints is knee pain. They're the most hard-working joints, subjected to a lot of wear and tear through the years.

With age, our ligaments and connected tissues gradually lose their elasticity and mobility. This brings discomfort and pain, especially while walking. Due to various factors, especially poor nutrition, the production and viscosity of the synovial liquid in the joints diminishes. This is a direct road to Arthrosis.

To prevent further inflammation and destruction there are natural recipes to strengthen your knees without medication and surgery. This oat drink is useful for anybody who suffers from knee pain. It strengthens synovial liquid production and improves the elasticity of ligaments in the joints. The ingredients are:

- 1 glass of water
- 50g of oat flakes
- 100ml of orange juice
- 1 tablespoon of crushed nuts
- 1 tablespoon of honey
- Cinnamon to taste

Cook the porridge using the oats and water as normal. Once it has cooled, mix in the rest of ingredients and blend. This cocktail is rich in nutrients that support the normalisation of the metabolism and synovial liquid production.

**What my Grandma taught me:**
*Mix carrot, sea buckthorn with honey – heal your ulcers of the legs.*

## Cabbage for bruises or inflammations of joints

An excellent method for the treatment of hematomas and sprains: dip a piece of wool in cabbage juice, squeeze and attach to the sore spot, secured with a bandage. Keep the compress until the fabric dries. Apply the wrap until the bruise disappears.

In the same way, gout, arthritis, arthrosis and bursitis are treated with a course of 1 to 3 months. Apply a compress to your joints daily for the night and get ready for the fact that the painful symptoms do not disappear immediately you will have to be patient. If you persevere, you will get a remarkable pain-relieving result.

# GENERAL HEALTH AND LONGEVITY

## Two Ingredients – 16 Healing Effects: castor oil and bicarbonate of soda

This mixture would rid you of back and knees pains, red eyes, fungus in nails and toes, warts, and a lot more.

YES, I am talking about universal mixture of castor oil and bicarbonate of soda. On top of its miraculous healing effects it is worth using for skin and hair care. See what it could do for you!

1. To reduce allergies, mix 3 tablespoons of soda with 1 tablespoon of castor oil, and spread it all over your body before the shower. Lightly massage it onto your skin, leave it there for a few minutes and then rinse it off. Also, drinking 5-7 drops of castor oil helps to fight allergy.

2. To get rid of fungus, mix 1 tablespoons of each, soda and castor oil, put it on your feet and nails, and leave it there for 30-40 minutes, then rinse them with warm water and dry well.

3. Use the above mixture to speed up healing in bruises, cuts and wounds.

4. The same mixture, applied to your knees overnight, will reduce or eliminate pain.

5. To prevent cataract put one drop of pure castor oil in your eyes before sleep.

6. For irritable and red eyes use a mask from 1 teaspoon of Castor oil and 0.5 teaspoon of soda. Apply it onto clean eyelids for 20 minutes and then carefully rinse it out with warm water. It also helps against dark circles and puffiness around the eyes.

7. Use that mixture for irritable and inflamed skin.

8. Also use it for massaging your feet to get rid of salt deposits in the joints.

9. Apply that mixture to your age spots on your hands. Do it regularly and watch them fading away.

10. To rejuvenate your hands 2-3 times a week make a mixture of equal amounts of castor oil and soda. Apply and massage your hands with it.

11. The same mixture should be used for neck massage. It takes time, but in a few weeks creases on your neck will smooth out, and also chronic pains disappears.

12. It also works against Papilloma. Apply it for 30-40 minutes, then rinse it out. Repeat regularly until they shrink and gradually disappear.

13. With warts it works faster. Apply the mixture directly on the wart, bandage it and keep it overnight. Repeat it in the morning, and keep repeating it until complete disappearance of the wart. That could happen in a matter of days.

14. This mixture could be helpful against pain and itch from insect bites.

15. 2 drops of castor oil a day into your ears help to eliminate ear ringing.

16. To stop hair loss and strengthen your hair, massage your scalp with castor oil before washing. It nurtures the scalp and encourages new growth.

## The Easiest Remedy to Rejuvenate Your Body in 40 Days

This is an old recipe and a potent mixture, based on only two ingredients. The first one is fig, an extremely good fruit for health, both fresh and dry. The best figs are those of a light, yellow colour. During the drying process, their healing properties multiply. The fig's natural proteins and sugars are easy to metabolise. Dried figs can significantly increase energy production, improve our mental activity, our mood and capacity to work.

Dried figs are also very rich in fibre, giving you a feeling of being full for a long time and improving digestion. They contain magnesium, iron, calcium and vitamin B. There is also a high amount of pectin in figs, which makes it an effective remedy for healing connective tissues, especially after joint and bone trauma. Another important component found in dried figs, rutin, works to strengthen capillaries.

Daily consumption of figs decreases the risk of developing cardiovascular conditions. The following recipe is age-old and has been used in various cultures for the rejuvenation of the body, the improvement of its physical and mental abilities and as a treatment for many ailments. The recipe is extremely simple—take 20 dried figs, cut each of them in two and place them in a glass jar. Add olive oil, covering the figs, plus ½ - 1 cm above. Refrigerate for 40 days and then it will be ready to use. Simply eat half a fig and take a teaspoon of the oil from the jar 5-10 minutes before breakfast. Continue until finished. You will feel the healing power of the remedy straight away. Repeat this 2-3 times a year.

## The Plant of "Eternal Youth"

*"When in doubt – use nettle".*
                                David Hoffman

This plant has been used in folk medicine for centuries for its incredible healing properties. It decreases sugar levels, cleanses the kidney, rejuvenates skin, stops hair loss, as well as treating respiratory conditions such as:

- Pneumonia
- Sore throat
- Asthma
- Seasonal allergies

The plant with a rich scope of healing applications is nettle—let's see what it's useful for.

**SKIN:** Nettle tea has antibacterial, nutritional, cleansing and stimulating effects on the skin. It also supports collagen production. This tea can be drunk with honey or used externally for rinsing your face, as an ingredient for facial masks or for making nettle ice.

**KIDNEYS:** Nettle is a great diuretic and detoxifies the kidneys. It is also said that nettle tea can prevent the formation of kidney stones.

**HAIR:** It prevents hair loss, treats dandruff and makes hair stronger and brighter.

**BLOOD CIRCULATION:** As nettle is rich in chlorophyll, it helps to control bad cholesterol and improves blood circulation.

**DIABETES:** Nettle tea works to decrease the sugar in your blood.

**PROSTATE:** It works against hyperplasia, or enlargement of the prostate. Nettle cleanses the prostate and prevents cancer.

This list could be expanded to include immune system support, fighting anaemia and fatigue, insomnia and stress-related conditions. All the varieties of nettle available are medicinal. To make nettle tea is simple. Bring 1 litre of pure water to the boil, add 1 tablespoon of dry nettle leaves and cover with a lid for at least 10 minutes. Then percolate, add honey if desired and drink up to 3 cups a day. You can also add some lemon and mint for better taste. Using nettle tea regularly is very beneficial in many ways.

## Lecithin, a super-charger for your brain

Amongst the staggering choice of supplements, trace-minerals and vitamin it is really hard to pick one, which would be the most important. But I can take the courage to say that Lecithin could get the first prize if we run a contest of that nature.

In simple terms, Lecithin improves memory, speech, and motor problems that affect balance and movement.

A breakthrough study done in 1975 at the Massachusetts Institute of Technology (MIT) found that a daily supply of Lecithin "improves brain chemical activity." In particular, they found that Lecithin supports brain activities such as learning, memory, motor coordination, sensory feedback, and sleep patterns.

Since then, many more studies and research have been conducted that confirm what the huge role played by Lecithin in human and animal metabolism, especially related to our brain.

According to Dianne Craft, MA, CNHP, "the greatest recent discovery is the use of lecithin to activate a sluggish mind and improve memory.

This very important fatty acid, Lecithin, helps the body digest and utilize the fats and oils that are critical in maintaining efficient brain and nerve function. .Your brain, if dried and analysed, would show a composition of about 30% of lecithin".

So, what is Lecithin?

Lecithin is a substance that is produced by the liver to ensure the organ functions properly. It can also be found in plants and animals. It plays a significant role in synthesizing vitamins and minerals,

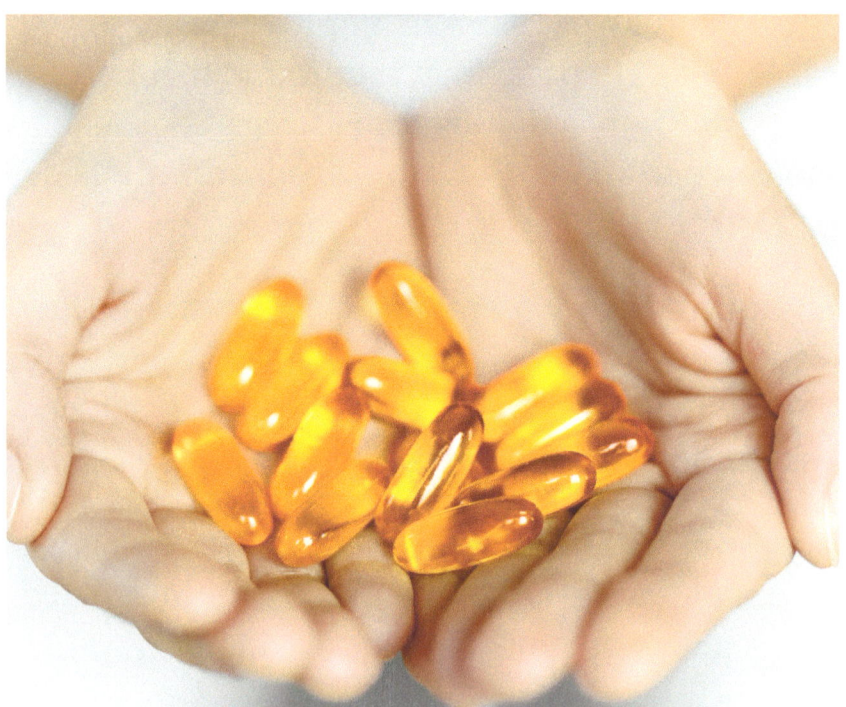

especially vitamins A, D, E and K. It is also essential for cell production and health because it assists cells to receive the nutrients they need.

Now that we know and understand the importance that Lecithin plays in the efficiency of our nervous system, brain processes, memory and motor function, many of us would like to add this important food to their daily diet.

You can find this substance in vegetables and legumes like various types of the vegetables from the cabbage family: broccoli, cauliflower, white and red cabbage, then many beans and legumes that are also rich in Lecithin, and most leafy veggies. Eggs, cheese, yoghurt, milk and other dairy products are also healthy sources of lecithin and many other useful nutrients. Soy is considered as one of the top sources of Lecithin.

However, it is hardly possible to measure its content in your food. Therefore, Lecithin as a supplement could give us some guarantee that we have it in a sufficient quantity. Since this is a food, one does not have to worry about taking too much lecithin.

Dianne Craft advised keeping the Lecithin supplement refrigerated once you have opened the container to keep it from becoming rancid. Lecithin should have a sweet, grainy odor when it is fresh. If it smells sour, it is not fresh.

You can improve emotional health, boost thinking powers of the brain, improve memory, and motor coordination by assuring that you and your children have an adequate number of needed neurotransmitters available at all times.

This is possible with the use of lecithin, the food your brain must have for total survival.

One interesting 'side effect' of Lecithin has been reported by several men. They noticed that, where their hairline had begun to recede, they discovered little tufts of new hair appearing.

Very promising, but it is still anecdotal evidence. More proof is needed, isn't it?

Dianne Craft suggested trying that fun science experiment at home. It will demonstrate the unique fat-dissolving ability of lecithin. If you sprinkle a tablespoon of lecithin granules on the cooled liquid from a beef roast you will see that the fat has been broken into many tiny particles as the lecithin emulsifies it.

That is a visual proof of how it works inside of your body by metabolising fats.

## Amazing study reveals more about Omega 3 fatty acids

**Omega-3s and Your Memory, Brain and Body**

Amazing study reveals more about Omega 3 fatty acids. If there weren't already enough health benefits to encourage you to add more Omega-3 to your diet, then perhaps the findings of Dr. Fuller-Looney's study published in the American Academy of Neurology's journal "Neurology" will do it. The study has found that not getting enough Omega-3s in your diet is responsible for problems related to your memory and thinking.

## About the Study

The study was conducted at the Easton Center for Alzheimer's Disease Research and the Division of Geriatrics, University of California in Los Angeles.

The researchers used 1,575 people of an average age of 67 who were free of dementia. They were given tests that measured their mental function as well as their body mass, along with MRI brain scans and tests to measure the amount of omega-3 fatty acids levels found in their red blood cells.

What they found was that the participants who had the lowest DHA levels had lower brain volume than the participants whose DHA levels were higher (DHA is an essential omega-3 fatty acid). The same was found for those who had the lowest omega-3 fatty acid levels, who went on to score lower on visual memory tests, as well as executive function tests such as those for problem solving, abstract thinking, and multi-tasking. They also noted that the participants with low omega-3 levels had brains that functioned as though they were two years older; showing that not getting enough omega-3s causes your brain to age faster.

**What Omega-3 Will Do For Your Brain and Body**

Omega-3 fatty acids have been found to positively impact your health on several different levels. Along with improving your memory and brain function, omega-3s have also been shown to lower the risk of heart disease and heart attack because of their ability to lower cholesterol, improve circulation, and reduce blood pressure.

Omega-3s are also known to lower the risk of certain cancers, including prostate, breast, and colon cancer. There have also been studies into the effects of omega-3 fish oils on rheumatoid arthritis and other inflammatory diseases, improved immune health, and even its impact on psychological disorders. Omega-3s are also crucial in your body's metabolism process and have been shown to lessen wrinkles and the signs of aging on the skin.

**How to Get Your Omega-3**

Along with several options for <u>omega-3 supplements</u>, you can increase the amount of omega-3s in your diet by incorporating foods that are rich in the nutrient, such as:

- Salmon
- Tuna
- Flaxseed
- Walnuts
- Olive and Canola oil
- Avocado

Incorporating these foods into your diet is a natural way to get the omega-3s you need for better health, and will ensure that you are doing everything you can to be the healthiest you can be!

# 11 CUCUMBER STORIES

A cucumber has been considered to be valuable food since Hippocrates' times. And it could top up any diet. But this vegetable has many other uses that you most likely did not know about.

## Cucumber story 1:

Do you know that a simple cucumber contains all the necessary vitamins and trace minerals: B1, B2, B3, B5, B6, Vit. C, Folic acid, Iron, Calcium, Phosphorus, Magnesium, Sodium and Zinc? It is also low calories and hydrated vegetable. Try to include it in your daily meals.

## Cucumber story 2:

When you feel tired in the afternoon, try this. Instead of pumping yourself with caffeine grab a cucumber. To restore alertness you need a product containing Vitamins of B group and carbs. All B vitamins are present in cucumbers, and – unexpectedly – also have some carbs. Eat one cucumber - and feel refreshed.

## Cucumber Story 3:

Are you tired of wiping the misted-out mirror in the bathroom after taking a shower? Before taking a bath, lubricate the mirror with a cucumber circle - it will not fog up, and the bathroom will have a pleasant smell.

## Cucumber Story 4:

If your garden is visited frequently by harmful insects, put cucumber slices in disposable Aluminium utensils. The combination of cucumber with Aluminium will cause a chemical reaction. As a result there will be a smell that the person does not feel, but for insects it is unbearable.

### Cucumber Story 5:

What to do if after taking alcohol you developed a very bad headache?

Do not drink more - first, and secondly, eat a cucumber and go to sleep. In the morning you wake up fresh, without a headache.

Cucumber contains both sugar and electrolyte, which together with vitamin B regulate the metabolism, disturbed by the acceptance of alcohol that caused you a headache.

### Cucumber Story 6:

Are you nervous before the exam? Take a cucumber, slice it and cover it with boiling water. Breathe the steam coming out of it and feel much calmer straight away.

**What my Grandma taught me:**
*Cucumber, carrot and beetroot juice - removing gall and kidney stones.*

### Cucumber Story 7:

You have an unpleasant smell from the mouth. Take a piece of cucumber and chew it for 30 seconds. The smell will disappear.

### Cucumber Story 8:

Taps, kitchen sink and gas stove need cleaning. Take a piece of cucumber and wipe the desired place several times.

The surface will not only glisten, but there will be no traces. In addition, your hands and nails will come into contact with natural material, not chemicals.

### Cucumber Story 9:

Did you write something with a pen and make a mistake?

Take the skin of the cucumber and gently erase the unnecessary letter. Cucumber can wipe even a felt-tip pen.

## Cucumber Story 10:

Cucumber has a cosmetic property to tighten the skin for a while. You are going to the swimming pool, but feel a bit embarrassed of cellulite on your legs? Take 1-2 circles of cucumber and smear these places with them. Wrinkles on the face will also be smoothed with cucumber for a while, and the skin becomes more elastic.

## Cucumber Story 11:

You have an important meeting, but you do not have time to polish your shoes? Take a cucumber circle and walk them on the surface of the shoes once. Your shoes immediately shine, like the new ones. In addition, the cucumber contains waterproof substances, and in case of rain, the feet will not get wet.

# 17 CABBAGE STORIES

We should not underestimate this leafy vegetable with a nickname "hundred clothes". The cabbage family members contain mineral salts (sulphur, calcium, potassium, phosphorus), fiber, lactase, lipase, sugar, anthocyanins, protease and other enzymes, phytoncides, vitamin A, vitamin B1, vitamin C. It possesses unique healing powers.

## Cabbage story 1:

Cabbage is the best product for weight loss, because it counteracts the formation of fat. Due to its rich chemical composition, cabbage holds a worthy place among the medicinal products of traditional medicine. Its antiseptic, anti-inflammatory, healing and vitamin properties are indisputable.

## Cabbage story 2:

Cabbage is a record holder in the number of nutrients in the composition. In addition to the standard fibre for vegetables, carbohydrates and proteins, it is rich in a complete set of essential amino acids that the body does not produce by itself, and therefore must get from food.

For an adult, 8 amino acids that are involved in the construction of proteins are indispensable; they are all present in the cabbage leaves.

## Cabbage story 3:

That's what happens if you put cabbage leaves to your leg for just 1 hour! If everything is done correctly, after just a day you will notice how the oedema disappears, the bruise has decreased, the swelling does not cause such strong painful sensations. After an evening spent wearing heels, there is no better solution for pain relief than cabbage wrapping.

**What my Grandma taught me:**
*Radiculitis bent you over – place cabbage leaves on painful zone.*

## Cabbage story 4:

How long to keep a compress from the cabbage leaf? During the day change the leaves for fresh every 2 hours to achieve the maximum therapeutic effect. And you can also leave them overnight.

## Cabbage story 5:

The cabbage compress is extremely effective as a means of decreasing pain, swelling and discomfort in varicose veins and inflammation of the joints, bruises and other injuries that are accompanied by oedema.

## Cabbage story 6:

Vitamin C (Ascorbigen) in cabbage lasts for 10 months and is not destroyed by heat and mechanical processing. The most important property of ascorbigen is the ability to suppress hormone-dependent cancer cells. Vitamin C is a chemical found in broccoli, cauliflower, cabbage, and related vegetables. It is used to make medicine. People take Ascorbigen for treating fibromyalgia and preventing breast cancer.

## Cabbage story 7:

How to prepare cabbage leaves for the compress.

1. Wash the cabbage, take off the top leaves. Blot the leaves with a napkin, cut the upper hard parts of them.
2. Wrap the leaves in foil and place them in the oven for 5 minutes to warm the leaves. The only point: they should not be hot! There is a risk that cabbage will lose its healing properties if overheated.
3. The prepared leaves wrap around the leg with a bandage.
4. For treating radiculitis and inflammation of the joints cabbage compress is recommended to do with honey.

## Cabbage story 8:

A compress with a cabbage leaf is a versatile healer. It could be used to treat Mastitis. The breast milk stagnation in lactating women could lead to inflammation and be a quite serious condition if not treated promptly. When the mammary glands swell and get hardened it is painful for women and difficult for a baby to suck on milk.

### Cabbage story 9:

Cabbage phytoncides are so powerful that they can kill pyogenic bacteria, which is capable of causing local inflammation containing puss. The so-called pyogenic cocci (many staphylococci, streptococci, and gonococci) and some other bacteria (the proteus, the pyocyanic, and anthrax groups, and sometimes even Bacillus coli) are pyogenic bacteria.

Cabbage phytoncides also kill Staphylococcus Aureus and Tuberculosis.

### Cabbage story 10:

When cutting the cabbage, throw away the stalk, do not give it to children. Study shows that the harmful nitrates accumulate in the stalk.

### Cabbage story 11:

Cabbage therapy, unlike anti-inflammatory tablets, will not lead to diseases of the digestive tract.

Brine from sauerkraut is the most well-known remedy for hangover. Thanks to its Vitamin C content, it quickly neutralizes alcohol toxins and speeds up the metabolism. Potassium in sauerkraut will bring back vigor and stimulate the work of the heart and other muscles.

## Cabbage story 12:

When there is no time to prepare the juice, you can simply attach a cabbage leaf to a bruise or an inflamed joint. That is how they were treated in ancient Rome.

Sometimes to enhance the therapeutic effect, honey or vegetable oil is spread on the skin under the cabbage leaf. The course of treatment: up to 3 months.

**Do not use honey on damaged skin.**

## Cabbage story 13:

The vitamins that make up the cabbage are exceptionally valuable products. A large amount of ascorbic acid, a natural antioxidant, strengthens bone, connective tissue and participates in metabolism. B vitamins are important for cell reproduction and the normal functioning of the nervous and immune systems. Nicotinic acid regulates redox processes (reduction and oxidation considered together as complementary processes) and the metabolism of fats and carbohydrates. Vitamin K provides the synthesis of proteins that affect blood coagulation. Vitamin E strengthens blood vessels and normalizes the endocrine system of the antioxidant

## Cabbage story 14:

Sauerkraut is a type of fermented cabbage with major health benefits as it is a storehouse of vitamins and nutrients. It is recommended to use for treating vitamin deficiency, intestinal lethargy and liver disease. The list of health benefits of sauerkraut is very long. So, I can only quote a few:

- Reduced overall inflammation including Arthritis inflammation
- Improvement of digestive disorders
- Improved immune system
- Prevention and symptom reduction of food allergies, including lactose intolerance, milk protein allergy and others
- Reduced risk of cancer
- Reduction of eczema symptoms
- Lowered cholesterol

There are many variations of sauerkraut recipes both in books and online. So, you can find them, make your choice and include it in your diet. You will be glad you did.

## Cabbage story 15:

Fresh cabbage juice is an excellent cosmetic that moisturizes the skin!

## Cabbage story 16:

Cabbage dishes are medicine! By consuming this vegetable, we stimulate many regenerative and recovery processes in the body. There are plenty of recipes for cabbage dishes that are easy to find in cookbooks and online. So, I only wish to draw your attention to sauerkraut. The recipe for sauerkraut originally came to us from China.

## Cabbage story 17:

Sciatica is a very painful condition. But natural help is available. In 500 ml of milk you need to cook 8 cabbage leaves until they are boiled soft. The resulting mass is spread on a piece of cotton fabric, applied to the lower back, fixed.

The procedure is repeated until inflammation has passed.

## Cabbage story 18:

For severe headache, make a mush of cabbage leaves, wrap them in a thin fabric and place it as a compress on the forehead and temples. And if you smear cabbage juice on your wrists and behind your ears, then the pain will pass even faster.

# More of My GRANDMA's medicine

## Lemon
- Glass of warm lemon water in the morning is effective detox
- Lemon juice is effective against spots and freckles
- Hot lemon tea with honey helps to reduce a fever and flu

**HOME REMEDIES**

## Chamomile
- Chamomile tea helps you fall asleep faster
- Chamomile tea is a wonderful remedy for headache
- Chamomile tea relieves PMS symptoms

## Peppermint
- Mint water soothes digestive tract
- Mint tea relieves nausea
- Mint leaves keep your mouth fresh

## Honey
- Honey and milk are good friends to better sleep
- Honey is a perfect natural exfoliator for your skin
- Honey is an effective home cure for insects bite

## Lavender
- Lavender tea gives you calm sleep
- Lavender aromatherapy reduces stress
- Lavender is natural insect repellant

- Why an apple a day? Pectin in apples reduces cholesterol.
- Drinking water before a meal – keeps you younger, longer.
- Apply an aspen (poplar) leaf where needed – it heals haemorrhoids.
- Drink beetroot juice – no stones in your liver.
- Want to be healthy all the time – care for the bees, not doctors.
- Feel under the weather? Eat garlic, mustard and lard.

- Cover burns with a slice of potato or grated carrot.
- The fractured bones heal faster if you eat ground eggs shells.
- Juniper berries' oil – heals the wounds.
- Hearing needs to strengthen up – drink Red Clover's decoction.
- Flu or cold – drink a decoction of linden and coltsfoot's flowers.
- Birch tree buds in vodka tincture – antiseptic best of all.
- Cucumber with carrot juice – put the roses on your cheeks.
- If sciatica is trouble – sleep in bed with a hot brick.
- Propolis with Acorus ("Sweet flag") in vodka - kills tooth pain in a bud.
- Suffering from haemorrhoids - no blood if carrot leaves' tea is in your cup.
- Propolis in alcohol with honey cures sore throat for long.
- Keep your splinter in kerosene – it gets loose as a hedgehog in a mud.

- Pain in legs – steam them over hot water with celandine herb in it.
- Soak rye bread in water and use this mask on your head – say Good Bye to dandruff.
- Diseases enter through the mouth.
- Look for your illness at the bottom of your plate.
- Eat in moderation – makes you stronger, and from a plentiful feed – shorter way to a grave.
- Drink tea - forget the longing.
- Buckwheat porridge - our mother, and a loaf of rye - our father.
- If there is cabbage in the barrel, there will be no trouble.
- Carrot improves blood: eat one carrot every day. And follow it up with a teaspoon of olive oil.

# BONUS STORIES

## Why are you not losing weight?

This is an old anecdote:

> The guy was in a prison, waiting for execution.
>
> He was taken to an electric chair but he was so grossly obese that could not fit into the chair.
>
> Then it was decided to make him lose weight, and then complete the execution.
>
> His daily food intake was reduced but he did not lose weight.
>
> Then his lunch and dinner were cancelled – he gained even more weight.
>
> Next, he was deprived of any feed, no food at all.
>
> The whole month passed.
>
> He continued to get bigger. In desperation, the prison stuff asked him:
>
> - What's happening? Why don't you lose weight?
>
> - I am not sure, - the guy said. – **May be because of my lack of motivation?**

That is exactly true: the power or lack of motivation is a decisive tool on the way to achieving your goal.

The motivation is the main factor in performing any activities. It provides for your goals' realisation.

But there is – unfortunately – another power that is even greater that motivation. It is a mighty antagonist to your motivation that sounds like that:

"The doubts about the attainability of the goal."

Even the strongest motivation ingloriously failed before such an opponent.

What can we do then? How not to allow doubts to take over the power?

One of the ways is to look at other people who have achieved great results in their life.

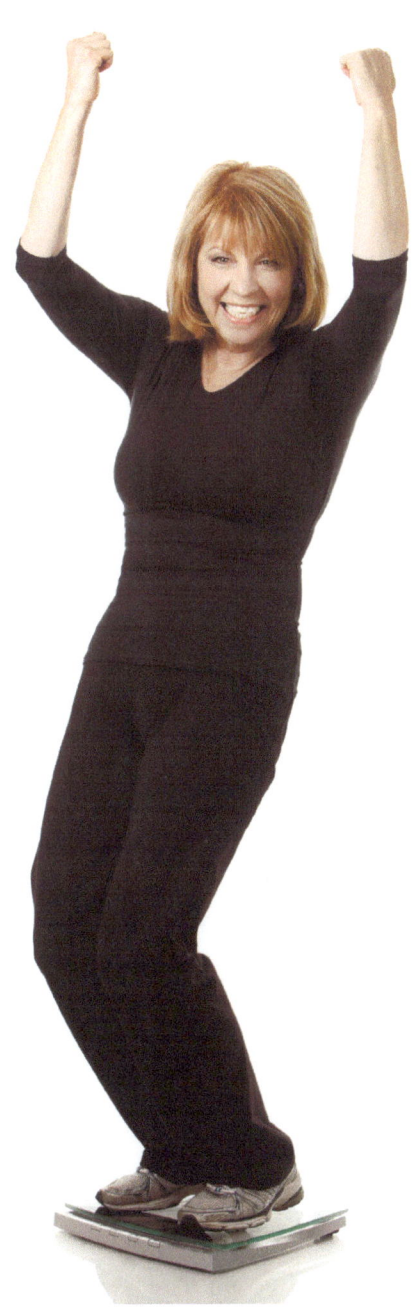

Let's start a discussion about how to conquer obesity.

I know, it's a bit f a jungle. It is a very commercialised area, the lucrative business for selling all sort of junk labelled 'miracles'.

However, let's see through the entangled web of heavy advertising and then have a look outside.

What do you see? Many overweight and obese people of all ages who, quite likely, spent fortunes on diets, tables, shakes, programs and courses, and what?

Why the crowd is still comprises of many big bottoms, heavy thighs, double chins, puffing persons who need to stop for a breather?

You know, the truth is in the pudding.

I am quite perplexed with how strong our desire is for miracles, for fairy-tale solutions; how deeply we believe that one day some guru comes and waives his magic wand, and - voila! –I look in the mirror and see myself size 12 instead of size 18! I love miracles, I am longing for magic, but... life taught me otherwise.

Therefore, wake up, girls and boys. For 20 years of sweet indulgence you accumulated your kilos and you wish to lose it in a month? In a week? Tomorrow?

My God! If you find out how to do it, tell me first. Please! Alas… The hard yakka is waiting.

What you need is a plan. A very detailed, concise, very well researched, based on your findings of solid evidence about how other people achieved their goal of losing weight.

If that sounds simple to you, think again. As soon as you take your pen and paper and start jotting what you have to do, you'll stumble, and not once, many times.

That is how the proper goal setting works.

I spent a lot of my professional time learning how to approach it, set it right and then get a result.

I describe the whole process in my book "The Lukin Longevity System" - where the setting of goals requires a systematic approach.

If you need help, please contact me. Wishing you best for your daring endeavours.

## Your body is a self-healing system

> *"Whether you think you can, or you think you can't - you're right."*
>
> Henry Ford

You shall trust me on that statement. Our world is changing rapidly, and so our view of it does. More and more people are coming to realisation that there is a close connection between what is happening in the person's mind and what is happening in his body and how it affects his perception of the reality of his surrounding environment.

The concept of our ability to heal ourselves is based on many ancient healing methods, observations and mantras coming from all lands and continents. And in the recent decades it has been numerously researched and confirmed by many scientists and doctors – again – from around the world.

- What does it mean to you personally?
- That means you could be in command of many processes in your body.

Don't take me wrongly. It is not a denial of medicine, not at all. Spiritual, visual and mental powerful techniques shall integrate with both traditional and alternative medicine beautifully. You probably come across those modern terms: integrative medicine and complementary medicine. That is where ancient and modern treatments meet and amalgamate with Eastern and Western approaches. Nowadays, official medicine recognise a power of meditation and positive mindset as the healing tools along with conventional practices.

So, let talk about what is 'mind over matter' in relation to what is self-healing, or more precisely – self-healing programming.

- How it works?
- What is the trigger mechanism to make it work?

It is rather simple: however, it requires systematic approach and perseverance.

Practice makes perfect, right? Lets do it.

We have to remind ourselves that our body, by the power of nature, could heal and repair itself by using own internal resources. You must convince yourself that you body, under no circumstances, would let you down.

Here it is – a very powerful affirmative phrase that is worth repeating a few times a day:

My body is a self-healing system, and I know that any pathologic process in my body is reversible.

Many people admitted that by the regular use of that mental formula they feel better both physically and mentally, their moods and feelings become optimistic and joyous, and energy level is lifted up.

If you are ready for the next step and wish to get rid of some bothering you conditions whether it is acute or chronic – that is an excellent mental exercise for your self-healing. I recommend you to do it twice a day: in the morning and at night, before sleep.

1. Close your eyes
2. Visualise a red colour ray of light, and
3. Direct it right into your blood vessels' system.

Try to observe how that red light is moving inside of your veins, vessels and capillaries, spreading throughout of all your body.

Imagine, how that red ray works in your body, saturating your blood and giving strength to all the organs and systems.

For this exercise to work it is compulsory for at least 2 minutes – not less – to keep focus on the only thought in your mind. That thought is:

My body has been healed, I am healthy, all my systems rejuvenate.

The total concentration on that thought is the key to success.

Those 2 minutes will work as a tonic for your health.

## The ageing of the human body begins in the legs, and that is why

Long ago, since ancient times, Chinese discovered it. That had been described in their manuscripts with the advice on how to strengthen the legs, and by doing that to postpone the body ageing.

Firstly, they insisted on the necessity to walk barefoot! Of course, we practically don't have a chance to do it in the street. Then do it at home. Even if you floor is cold, never mind, take off your slippers and socks and give it at least 10 minutes. If you will be persistent enough and do it 2-3 times a day – congratulations! You are going to live longer, and your ageing has been delayed!

It is important to vary your movements: walk a bit on your heels, then on your toes, and also on the outer and inner parts of your feet. That makes your feet stronger, strengthens your muscles and bones, hence, it improves blood circulation in them. In turn, your internal organs also function better.

Honestly, it's not a complex task, and only laziness could stop you from doing it. Start right now!

Then another super useful exercise: lightly beat your feet, from today – daily. That shall be done in a gentle manner, right behind your toes. You can use for this some small rubber or timber hammer, or even an empty bottle. Pretty soon you start feeling how pleasant warmth is spreading through your body, and you become more relax and calm.

That simple exercise is considered one of the best ones to improve blood circulation firstly in your leg, and then in the whole body. Interestingly, for people with vision problems, has been found to be effective to do that 'beating' right behind $2^{nd}$ and $3^{rd}$ toes, just for 5 minutes but every day. Those are the reflex zones, associated with the eyes.

Even nowadays, Chinese doctors are convinced that by massaging a special spot on the feet on a regular basis also supports better circulation and relaxation in the legs muscles.

They call that acupuncture point Yun-Tsyuan, which is located in the middle on the foot's arch. They are offering two methods of doing it: the dry one and the wet one. The dry one is just to press that spot 20 times without break, first on one foot, then on the other, not pressing too much. They suggest one has to do it twice a day: in the morning and in the evening.

For using a wet method: prepare a basin with 38C (roughly) water, place your feet in there and wait until they get red. Then, using your thumbs press and massage the spot 80 times with no break. Then rub the feet up for a few minutes.

## The Mona Lisa Smile

> *"Smiling is definitely one of the best beauty remedies. If you have a good sense of humour and a good approach to life, that's beautiful".*
> Rashida Jones

The internal smile, also known as The Mona Lisa Smile, is a very powerful practice of healing, originating from ancient China. Many people spend their lives experiencing anger, sadness, depression, fear, anxiety and other kinds of negative energy. These energies cause chronic illness and drain our vitality. The internal smile is sincere, emanating from the whole body, including all organs, glands, muscles, bones and the nervous system. It produces high-quality energy that can heal and eventually transform itself into even higher quality energy.

A sincere smile sends a loving energy that has the power to heal and transform. Remember a time

when you were upset or physically ill; someone, perhaps even a stranger smiled sincerely and - suddenly you felt better. The internal smile directs loving energy into our organs and glands, which is necessary for healing and good life. The internal smile is the best medicine for neutralising any kind of stress.

*"The internal smile is sincere, emanating from the whole body, including all organs, glands, muscles, bones and the nervous system."*

## 11 steps to practice internal smile

1. Sit comfortably and keep your spine in an upright position—relax.

2. Take a couple of slow, deep breaths noticing how your abdomen rises and relax with each breath.

3. Rest the tip of your tongue gently on the roof of your mouth.

4. Smile gently, allowing your lips to feel full and smooth as they spread to the side and lift just slightly.

5. Now bring your attention to the space between your eyebrows—your "third eye". Focus on this centre and feel gentle vibrations there.

6. Bring your attention now to the centre of your brain. This is a place referred to in Taoism as the "crystal palace". Feel the energy gathering in the middle of your head.

7. Allow this energy to flow forward into your eyes. Feel your eyes "smiling".

8. Now, direct the energy of your smiling eyes back and down into someplace in your body where you need healing, where you've recently had an injury or illness.

9. Continue to smile into that place within your body and let it absorb this energy like a sponge soaking up nourishing water.

10. When this feels complete, direct your inner smile into your solar plexus.

11. Release the tip of your tongue from the roof of your mouth and let the smile go.

When your energy grows, you will become more flexible and adaptable. You will know what you want in life and how to achieve it.

## Support for your vision

Three rules that can help you to keep your vision in good condition.

### Rule Number 1. Use your eyes fully.

Perfect vision function for both - far and near sight – is a part of our brain design. Therefore, ideally as much time as you work in the near-sight area, roughly the same time is recommended to spend looking into distance. And never forget to give your eyes a rest.

### Rule Number 2. 45 minutes at one range of vision

Performing monotonic task like working on computer, reading a book, watching TV every 45 minutes your eyes need break. That is a standard time for a school lesson, based on science. Never mind how busy you are, just stop doing what you are doing, and follow Rule Number 3.

## Rule Number 3. Exercise and relax

After using your eyes for intensive work, stand up, exercise your shoulders and neck for a few minutes and then sit for a short while with closed eyes providing relaxation for the eye muscles. If your eyes work hard and never properly relax that leads to the gradual vision impairment.

To summarise the book up I wish to share with you a few inspirational quotes related to your health.

\* \* \*

*"Nature itself is the best physician"*

Hippocrates

*"Let us permit the nature to have her way. She understands her business better than we do"*

Michel Montaigne

www.ingramcontent.com/pod-product-compliance
Lightning Source LLC
Chambersburg PA
CBHW041823220426
43666CB00004BA/57